Shel Silverstein

WHO WROTE THAT?

LOUISA MAY ALCOTT

JANE AUSTEN

AVI

JUDY BLUME

BETSY BYARS

MEG CABOT

BEVERLY CLEARY

ROBERT CORMIER

BRUCE COVILLE

ROALD DAHL

CHARLES DICKENS

THEODOR GEISEL

WILL HOBBS

ANTHONY HOROWITZ

GAIL CARSON LEVINE

C.S. LEWIS

ANN M. MARTIN

L.M. MONTGOMERY

PAT MORA

WALTER DEAN MYERS

SCOTT O'DELL

BARBARA PARK

GARY PAULSEN

TAMORA PIERCE

EDGAR ALLAN POE

BEATRIX POTTER

PHILIP PULLMAN

MYTHMAKER: THE
STORY OF J.K.
ROWLING

MAURICE SENDAK

SHEL SILVERSTEIN

GARY SOTO

R.L. STINE

EDWARD L.
STRATEMEYER

E.B. WHITE

LAURA INGALLS
WILDER

LAURENCE YEP

JANE YOLEN

Shel Silverstein

Michael Gray Baughan

Foreword by
Kyle Zimmer

CHELSEA HOUSE
PUBLISHERS
An imprint of Infobase Publishing

Shel Silverstein

Chelsea House
An imprint of Infobase Publishing
132 West 31st Street
New York NY 10001

Library of Congress Cataloging-in-Publication Data
Baughan, Michael Gray, 1973-
  Shel Silverstein / Michael Gray Baughan.
      p. cm. — (Who wrote that?)
  Includes bibliographical references and index.
  ISBN-13: 978-0-7910-9676-5 (acid-free paper) 1. Silverstein, Shel—
Juvenile literature. 2. Authors, American—20th century—Biography—
Juvenile literature. 3. Children's literature—Authorship—Juvenile literature.
4. Illustrators—United States—Biography—Juvenile literature. 5. Composers—
United States—Biography—Juvenile literature. I. Title.
  PS3569.I47224Z55 2008
  818'.5409—dc22
  [B]   2007045336

Chelsea House books are available at special discounts when purchased in bulk quantities for business, associations, institutions, or sales promotions. Please call our Special Sales Department in New York at (212) 967-8800 or (800) 322-8755.

You can find Chelsea House on the World Wide Web at http://www.chelseahouse.com

Text design by Keith Trego and Erika Arroyo
Cover design by Keith Trego and Jooyoung An

Printed in the United States of America

Bang EJB 10 9 8 7 6 5 4 3 2 1

This book is printed on acid-free paper.

Table of Contents

FOREWORD BY
KYLE ZIMMER
PRESIDENT, FIRST BOOK

HUMANITY IS POWERED by stories. From our earliest days as thinking beings, we employed every available tool to tell each other stories. We danced, drew pictures on the walls of our caves, spoke, and sang. All of this extraordinary effort was designed to entertain, recount the news of the day, explain natural occurrences—and then gradually to build religious and cultural traditions and establish the common bonds and continuity that eventually formed civilizations. Stories are the most powerful force in the universe; they are the primary element that has distinguished our evolutionary path.

Our love of the story has not diminished with time. Enormous segments of societies are devoted to the art of storytelling. Book sales in the United States alone topped $24 billion in 2006; movie studios spend fortunes to create and promote stories; and the news industry is more pervasive in its presence than ever before.

There is no mystery to our fascination. Great stories are magic. They can introduce us to new cultures or remind us of the nobility and failures of our own; inspire us to greatness or scare us to death; but above all, stories provide human insight on a level that is unavailable through any other source. In fact, stories connect each of us to the rest of humanity not just in our own time, but also throughout history.

This special magic of books is the greatest treasure that we can hand down from generation to generation. In fact, that spark in a child that comes from books became the motivation for the creation of my organization, First Book, a national literacy program with a simple mission: to provide new books to the most disadvantaged children. First Book has been at work in hundreds of communities for over a decade. Every year, children in need receive millions of books through our organization, and millions more are provided through dedicated literacy institutions across the United States and around the world. In addition, groups of people dedicate themselves tirelessly to working with children to share reading and stories in every imaginable setting from schools to the streets. Of course, this Herculean effort serves many important goals. Literacy translates to productivity and employability in life and many other valid and even essential elements. But at the heart of this movement are people who love stories, love to read, and want desperately to ensure that no one misses the wonderful possibilities that reading provides.

When thinking about the importance of books, there is an overwhelming urge to cite the literary devotion of great minds. Some have written of the magnitude of the importance of literature. Amy Lowell, an American poet, captured the concept when she said, "Books are more than books. They are the life, the very heart and core of ages past, the reason why men lived and worked and died, the essence and quintessence of their lives." Others have spoken of their personal obsession with books, as in Thomas Jefferson's simple statement: "I live for books." But more compelling, perhaps, is the almost instinctive excitement in children for books and stories.

Throughout my years at First Book, I have heard truly extraordinary stories about the power of books in the lives of children. In one case, a homeless child, who had been bounced from one location to another, later resurfaced—and the only possession that he had fought to keep was the book he was given as part of a First Book distribution months earlier. More recently, I met a child who, upon receiving the book he wanted, flashed a big smile and said, "This is my big chance!" These snapshots reveal the true power of books and stories to give hope and change lives.

As these children grow up and continue to develop their love of reading, they will owe a profound debt to those volunteers who reached out to them—a debt that they may repay by reaching out to spark the next generation of readers. But there is a greater debt owed by all of us—a debt to the storytellers, the authors, who have bound us together, inspired our leaders, fueled our civilizations, and helped us put our children to sleep with their heads full of images and ideas.

WHO WROTE THAT? is a series of books dedicated to introducing us to a few of these incredible individuals. While we have almost always honored stories, we have not uniformly honored storytellers. In fact, some of the most important authors have toiled in complete obscurity throughout their lives or have been openly persecuted for the uncomfortable truths that they have laid before us. When confronted with the magnitude of their written work, we can forget that writers are people. They struggle through the same daily indignities and dental appointments, and they experience the intense joy and bottomless despair that many of us do. Yet, somehow they rise above it all to weave a powerful thread that connects us all. It is a rare honor to have the opportunity that these books provide to share the lives of these extraordinary people. Enjoy.

Shel Silverstein grew up in Chicago, Illinois, in the 1930s. In 1933, Chicago hosted the World's Fair, which that year was called the Century of Progress International Exhibition. Above is a panoramic view of the fair.

1

The Multitalented Misfit

LIKE THE LIVES they document, most biographies begin with a birth. This one will be no exception, but let me explain a few things first. Shel Silverstein managed to become relatively famous without revealing very much about himself. In fact, although at least 20 million copies of his books were sold, Silverstein remains a mystery.

With a few exceptions, Silverstein gave his last "real" interview in 1975. Early in his career, he specifically requested that his publisher withhold information about him. Silverstein's birth date is a perfect example: A new Web site established in his name (www.shelsilverstein.com) does not mention it. A substantial number of sources claim that he was born in 1932, which led to incorrect calculations of his age at the time of his death. No one knows whether this was the result of a mistake or misprint somewhere along the line, or a deliberate fib on Silverstein's part.

Fortunately, through the efforts of Carol Arnett and Sarah Weinman, creators of two key Silverstein Web sites, as well as biographer Lisa Rogak, author of *A Boy Named Shel: The Life and Times of Shel Silverstein,* some of these details have been clarified once and for all. Many large holes remain, however. If you step into one of these holes and get stuck, feel free to use your imagination to find a way out. Silverstein probably would have wanted it that way.

It would be somewhat counterproductive to write a standard, linear narrative of Silverstein's life and career, even if one could come up with a moment-by-moment timeline with all the pertinent dates, places, and names. Silverstein was a creative dynamo who worked in many different kinds of media, so he evades every attempt at categorization. In some ways, it is easier to think of him as five or six different artists who just happened to coexist in the same body. As such, and in the interests of narrative coherence, many of the chapters that follow are organized around one particular career path or body of work. Some chapters trace his life chronologically, and some do not. Mix and match them as your spirit moves you. Silverstein certainly did.

THE VIEW FROM THE DUGOUT

Sheldon Allan Silverstein was, in fact, born on September 25, 1930, in Chicago, Illinois, to Nathan and Helen Silverstein. Their daughter, named Peggy, was born four years later. Sheldon Silverstein grew up in Logan Square, a working-class neighborhood on the northwest side of the city, which had been settled by immigrants in the early 1900s.

Chicago, like the rest of the country, struggled to free itself from the shadow cast by the Great Depression. It organized the "Century of Progress" World's Fair, held in the city in 1933 and 1934. More than 39 million people attended, and it was the first event to pay for itself in ticket sales. The fair primarily showcased new technologies and promised attendees that a prosperous, equitable America lay just over the horizon. At the same time, the first-ever baseball All-Star Game was held at Comiskey Park in 1933. Chicago offered plenty of other distractions as well, from some of the nation's premier jazz clubs located on the South Side to the uptown theaters, ballrooms, and restaurants that were second only to New York's Time Square.

Not much is known about Silverstein's early childhood. He began to draw unusual pictures at a very young age, and he wrote stories and poems to accompany them. Although Silverstein was not much of an athlete himself, he became a devoted fan of the Chicago White Sox baseball team. As a teenager, he sold hot dogs and drinks at Comiskey Park, just so he could get in free to watch every game. He was both an artist and a sports fan, and these two sides of his personality helped to shape his self-image. In one of his few candid interviews, for *Publishers Weekly* in 1975, he said,

> When I was a kid—12, 14, around there—I would much rather have been a good baseball player or a hit with the girls. But I couldn't play ball, couldn't dance. Luckily, the girls didn't want me; not much I could do about that. So, I started to draw and to write. . . . By the time I got to where I was attracting girls, I already was into work and it was more important to me.[1]

Silverstein, from an early age, played the part of the misfit: someone who sat in the dugout, someone who drew pictures and watched while the other kids played ball, and someone for whom the imagination provided a safe haven. It is a point of view that shows up everywhere in Silverstein's writings and drawings. We shall return to this theme many times in the pages that follow.

FROM ART SCHOOL TO ARMY LIFE

Silverstein attended and graduated from Roosevelt High School. He went on to study art at the University of Illinois at Navy Pier, but he lacked focus and was dismissed from the school for poor performance. He enrolled at the Chicago Academy of Fine Arts and studied there for a year, then moved on to Roosevelt University, where he majored in English and completed three years of coursework before he was drafted into the army in 1953.

After he trained at Fort Riley in Kansas and Fort Belvoir in Virginia, Silverstein shipped out to serve in the Korean War. Surprisingly, his talents really flourished in the military. Given the army's demands for conformity and submission to authority (two things Silverstein was simply incapable of), one might guess his military service would have been a miserable period in his life. This was simply not the case. Later, in the introduction for *Grab Your Socks!* (the paperback reprint of *Take Ten*, his first book of cartoons), he would go so far as to say "the army was good to me. . . . I was given almost complete freedom to say what I had to say."[2]

The army provided Silverstein with two life-changing opportunities: the chance to travel and an outlet for his creative energies. Stationed first in Japan and later in Korea, Silverstein must have caught the eye of someone in authority

Silverstein was drafted into the army in 1953, and was assigned to the staff of the Stars and Stripes, *a military newspaper still in existence today. That is where he began his career as a cartoonist. Above, two servicemen read the issue of* Stars and Stripes *reporting the end of the Korean War.*

who was savvy enough to recognize that his personality was incompatible with combat training. Almost immediately, Silverstein was assigned to the staff of the Pacific edition of the *Stars and Stripes*, a newspaper for military personnel. This lucky turn of events not only saved him from the drudgery of training and potential danger of actual fighting, it also gave him a chance to do what he loved most.

Overnight, Silverstein had become a professional cartoonist. "For a guy of my age and with my limited experience to suddenly have to turn out cartoons on a day-to-day deadline, the job was enormous," he later admitted. "It was a great opportunity for me and I blossomed."[3] Even more important, he had the chance to experience new cultures and expand his horizons, which he apparently valued more highly than any of the education he had received back home. Of his aborted college experience he would later comment, "Imagine—four years you could have spent traveling around Europe meeting people, or going to the Far East of Africa or India, meeting people, exchanging ideas, reading all you wanted to anyway, and instead I wasted it at Roosevelt."[4]

Despite the latitude he was given, Silverstein still found himself in hot water with his superiors now and then. As a soldier, he was virtually hopeless when it came to discipline and following regulations. One day, some military policemen, who kept a special eye on him, found Silverstein wearing silly argyle socks with his uniform rather than the regulation solid-color socks and threatened to haul him in to be disciplined.

On staff at the *Stars and Stripes*, Silverstein's off-key style and irreverent humor created an uneasy tension at the office, and several of his cartoons did, in fact, draw fire. One depicted a woman and child in altered military uniforms, which suggested that quartermasters had stolen from the depot to clothe their families. Another criticized army food. As a result of these two cartoons in particular, Silverstein ran afoul of the Uniform Code of Military Justice (a code of law specific to the U.S. military) and, in both cases, nearly earned a court martial. Each time he found himself in trouble, however, Silverstein was able to talk his way out of it.

In 1955, the *Stars and Stripes* sponsored Silverstein's first book, *Take Ten*, which was later reprinted in paperback as *Grab Your Socks!* Printed in Tokyo, this collection of cartoons about army life contained many that were originally published in the newspaper, as well as some from his "untapped top drawer." It also featured a foreword by fellow soldier Robert D. Sweeney that provides a rare glimpse of the young cartoonist at work. Sweeney quotes a letter by Bob Brown, another *Stars and Stripes* staff member, about Silverstein:

> He stays up all night chewing pencils, drawing cartoons and writing ideas on little scraps of paper he never finds again. In the first twenty minutes he was here, he had our little office more cluttered than the convention hall in his native Chicago. . . . But he knows the people he draws. He's lived through the same experiences and heard the same lines. In Korea, he has spent his time up front in the outposts and the squad tents with the fellows he wanted most to please.[5]

This empathy that Bob Brown describes—Silverstein's ability to find humor in a given situation or subject, while still still able to treat it with honesty and compassion—is a key component to his greatness, both as an artist and as a human being. Silverstein was always laughing *with* his fellow soldiers, as opposed to *at* them. "It's been said that through my drawings I was trying to take a poke at the army. This is not so," he later said. "There was a lot about the military that I thought was pretty silly—and I enjoyed kidding those things because I knew the guys felt the same way—but these cartoons weren't meant to take a poke at anybody or anything. They were meant to make people laugh."[6] No doubt that laughter helped many a man get through a hard day.

AT HOME AND AT LARGE

Silverstein returned home on leave to Chicago in 1955 and managed to get some work as a cartoonist for *Look* magazine and *Sports Illustrated*. Upstart publisher Hugh Hefner saw Silverstein's work, and he instantly recognized its creator as a fellow fun-loving hipster. He not only invited Silverstein to draw for his fledging *Playboy* magazine, he also offered him an executive suite at the Playboy mansion. Silverstein would continue to publish cartoons, articles, and excerpts from his books in *Playboy* for the next 25 years, and he and Hefner became lifelong friends.

The following year, Silverstein began to write travel pieces for *Playboy* from various stops on his wayward journeys. First he wrote from Tokyo, where he had returned to his army service, then various European locales. After his discharge in 1959 he dispatched from Africa, and finally, Alaska and Hawaii in 1961. When he was in Africa, he suffered a badly broken leg in a car accident and was forced to return home for a while. It was sometime during this period that he began to write songs.

A MUSICIAN, TOO?

In 1959, the world was treated to the release of Silverstein's first music record. The project was the result of a stage show put together by Jean Shepard, a good friend and oddball radio personality. A quartet called the Red Onion Jazz Band provided musical accompaniment to a variety of acts, and Silverstein sang along.

Later that year, the same group entered the studio and recorded the album *Hairy Jazz*. The silly spirit of the effort is revealed in the album's liner notes, written by Shepard, which describe Silverstein as a famous actor and opera singer, who "overnight . . . took his place among the all time greats of the operatic world" before he had an "unfortunate accident."[7] If the listener overlooked Shepard's ironic introduction to Silverstein's peculiar brand of singing, song titles like "Good Whiskey" and "Kitchen Man" left little room for doubt. That same year, Silverstein would return the favor when he wrote the liner notes for Shepard's album, *Jean Shepard and Other Foibles*, in which he depicts Shepard as a heroic fugitive caught up in all sorts of international intrigues.

Silverstein would go on to record and release 8 more original albums and write nearly 800 songs. Just recently, there has been a renewed interest in these albums, and several of them have been rereleased on CD. Although they are full of whimsy and humor, the CDs contain mostly adult material; anyone who expects children's music will be in for a rude shock. In Chapter 4, we will explore more of this largely unknown aspect of his career.

"NOT FOR CHILDREN, OF WHATEVER AGE"

In 1960, Silverstein completed *Now Here's My Plan: A Book of Futilities*. This book collected many of the cartoons first published in *Playboy*, and it provides an early glimpse at the visual style that Silverstein would later use in his most famous works. As Ruth MacDonald points out in her excellent book, *Shel Silverstein*:

> [T]hough this early work has no *direct* bearing on the children's books, there are two obvious influences. First, the cartoons' captions all use a typeface that resembles that of a typewriter. . . . The same typewriter font is found in nearly all his children's books, to greatest effect in the volumes of poetry, in which the font's wide, open look and the extra spacing between letters make the books easy to read.

MacDonald goes on to say:

The second influence is the cartoon medium itself. . . . Silverstein experimented with framing an illustration and with the use of a limited space to convey his point. . . . The lack of a frame around an illustration in a picture book suggests an experience that is easily entered into and that totally engages the reader. . . . His illustrational style in the children's books is remarkably light, with little shading or crosshatching; the page's airy appearance . . . invites the viewer/reader into the experience.[8]

Now Here's My Plan takes its title from the caption of Silverstein's most famous early cartoon, which depicts two dying prisoners manacled to a wall in a dungeon, with no chance of escape. Despite their hopeless predicament, one of them somehow finds the optimism to whisper those four words to his brother in suffering. The cartoon is emblematic of both Silverstein's black humor and his faith in the power of the imagination.

What is most interesting about *Now Here's My Plan*, however, is the foreword by Jean Shepard, Silverstein's

Did you know...

According to Silverstein's pal Rik Elswit, the famous "Now Here's My Plan" cartoon has an unpublished sequel, drawn privately for a friend. The same bleak prison scene is depicted, but in the sequel, the manacles are empty.

playful pal. In one of the most ironic statements ever made about an artist, Shepard says "[s]ince Shel Silverstein is a close friend of mine, I would very much like to be able to recommend him to everyone without reservation of any kind. This I cannot do. For one thing, he is not for children, of whatever age."[9]

In the next chapter, we will see how Silverstein had to be persuaded to write for children, first by his friend Tomi Ungerer, and then by powerhouse editor Ursula Nordstrom. We get the sense that Shepard made an inside joke here; perhaps it was a reference to a private conversation between the two of them on the subject. Given the outrageous liner notes they once wrote for each other, we should not take Shepard's comment too seriously. It does underscore the fact, however, that nothing in Silverstein's work up to that point would suggest that he would go on to become one of the all-time most popular authors of literature for children.

As in Sweeney's introduction to *Take Ten*, Shepard's foreword to *Now Here's My Plan* includes some juicy details about Silverstein's personal habits. Shepard describes both the cartoonist's style of dress and his apartment as sloppy, but full of character and originality. He calls Silverstein "the only continuously funny man I have ever known" and auspiciously suggests that, if only he were to lock himself in a room with "a supply of paper and ink, his banjo, and a radio to hear the ball games," Silverstein would almost certainly "turn out the great body of work that is in him."[10]

In 1960, Silverstein continued his work for *Playboy* with a series of extended pieces he called "Teevee Jeebies." These are old movie stills (pictures of scenes from movies), to which he added funny new captions. Thirty years later, the producers at the Comedy Channel would use a very similar premise to create the hit show *Mystery Science Theater 3000*. Silverstein made enough of these parodies to publish two book-length collections, *Playboy's Teevee Jeebies* (1963) and *More Playboy's Teevie Jeebies: Do-It-Yourself Dialogue for the Late Late Show* (1965).

MEET YOUR UNCLE SHELBY

The following year, in 1961, Silverstein traveled to Alaska and Hawaii, and again logged his experiences for *Playboy*. He also wrote and published *Uncle Shelby's ABZ: A Primer for Tender Young Minds*. This black-humored parody of ABC books reads as if it were deliberately written to sabotage Silverstein's potential career as a children's author. Uncle Shelby was a persona, or an alias, that Silverstein occasionally adopted, which allowed him to tell his stories with a sly wink and break the rules a little bit without getting into too much trouble.

Many families include at least one rascally uncle with a tendency to encourage bad behavior in his nephews or nieces and to subvert the authority of their parents. If that uncle were a stranger, the parents would be furious, but because he is a family member and because he is often a good storyteller, he is given a little more latitude. In the case of *Uncle Shelby's ABZ*, this naughtiness is decidedly mean-spirited; little children are advised to eat unripe apples and drink black ink, among other things. As a result, the humor is really only appropriate for adults, or possibly much older children who have developed the ability to tell when someone is teasing them.

Over the years, *Uncle Shelby's ABZ* has become somewhat notorious as the "early Silverstein classic you won't want your children to read." When it was reprinted in 1985, it had the previous quote on the back and a new subtitle:

"A Primer for Adults Only." In 1961, however, Uncle Shelby's antics did not represent a departure for Silverstein; they were merely a continuation of the adult material he had published in *Playboy* and elsewhere. Jean Shepard's assessment that he was "not for children" was still quite accurate. That would change, however, with the publication of Silverstein's next book and the beginning of his lifelong collaboration with editor Ursula Nordstrom.

Shel Silverstein was photographed in New York City in 1973, 10 years after he wrote Lafcadio, The Lion Who Shot Back, *under the editorial direction of Ursula Nordstrom.*

2

The Zookeeper

IF YOU ARE a fan of Shel Silverstein's books for children, you have Tomi Ungerer to thank for it. It was Ungerer, a good friend of Silverstein's and a fellow author/illustrator, who first suggested that he entertain kids. At first, Silverstein was not too keen on the idea: "[Tomi] practically dragged me, kicking and screaming, into Ursula Nordstrom's office. And she convinced me that Tomi was right; I could do children's books."[1]

You should certainly thank Ursula Nordstrom, as well. Ursula Nordstrom was easily one of the most influential people in twentieth-century children's literature. From 1940 to 1973,

"Ursa Major," as she was affectionately called by one author,[2] was the editorial director of Harper's Department of Books for Boys and Girls (now HarperCollins Children's). Her credits read like a list of the genre's greatest works, including *Charlotte's Web*, *Where the Wild Things Are*, *The Runaway Bunny*, *Harold and the Purple Crayon*, and *Goodnight Moon*.

Clearly, Nordstrom had a keen eye for the kind of books that would become perennial bestsellers. It must have boosted Silverstein's confidence immensely to learn that this publishing prophet foresaw such greatness in him. More important, Nordstrom was the right kind of editor for Silverstein. She championed unconventional books that were honest to children instead of the "happily ever after" stories that had dominated the genre for so long. Her private motto, which was "good books for bad children,"[3] also suited Silverstein. The fact that few people outside the publishing industry know Nordstrom's name is evidence of yet another trait she shared with Silverstein: the desire to let the books speak for themselves.

LAFCADIO

Silverstein's first effort for Nordstrom was *Lafcadio, the Lion Who Shot Back*, which was published in 1963. The book tells the story of a lion who, unlike his friends, refuses to run when a hunter starts to shoot at him one day. The lion instead tries to reason with the hunter, but the man will not listen, and so the lion eats him and takes his gun. In time, the lion learns to shoot like a man and to shoot back at anyone who threatens him. In fact, he becomes such a crack shot that he is invited to leave his jungle home and join the circus. The circus man gives him the name Lafcadio.

Although Silverstein never said so, the name was likely taken from *Lafcadio's Adventures*, a satire by the French novelist Andre Gidé, in which a poor young man is transformed into a wealthy aristocrat.

When Lafcadio enters the "civilized" company of humans, he becomes less like a lion and more like a man: He takes a bath, dresses in a suit, gets a haircut, and eats in a restaurant. Along the way, Lafcadio makes many humorous mistakes, but he always gets his way when he scares people with his roar. As word of his fame spreads, Lafcadio becomes Lafcadio the Great and travels all over the world. He experiences the best things that human life has to offer, but he becomes bored and unsatisfied. "Everything isn't everything," he tells Uncle Shelby, who serves as the story's narrator. The circus man suggests that he go on a hunting trip. Lafcadio comes full circle on the hunt when he encounters an old lion that reminds him of what he really is. Caught between life as a man and life as a lion, Lafcadio cannot decide what to do, so he heads off to live on his own.

Three things about *Lafcadio* establish a model for all of Silverstein's works to come. They also help explain why so many children like to read his books. First, the ending is ambiguous; it does not tell the reader what to think or how to feel. Silverstein trusts the reader to make up his or her own mind. This is a welcome change for many children, who spend much of their young lives being lectured to by their parents.

Second, the style of the text is vernacular, which means that it mimics the informal way that people really talk. This makes the reader or listener, as the case may be, feel less intimidated and more likely to want to continue with the book. Finally, the narrator talks directly to the child and includes him or her in the story; at one point, Silverstein even claims to have seen the reader walk by a barbershop window. All of these things give his books the feel of a secret chat with a rascally uncle who tells you things that other adults will not.

OPENING UP ON THE AIR

As he put the finishing touches on *Lafcadio*, Silverstein was invited to do a radio show with Studs Terkel, a prominent radio personality in Chicago, who later became one of the most prolific interviewers in American history. The broadcast, as well as Silverstein's follow-up appearance on the show in 1963, was more like a conversation than a formal interview. It was one of the few times Silverstein truly opened up and spoke unguardedly to the media about his influences, his contemporaries, and a whole range of other subjects.

In the interview, Silverstein was revealed as a dynamic nonconformist who raged against anything and everything

Did you know...

Lafcadio was published the same year as Maurice Sendak's classic book *Where the Wild Things Are*. It is interesting how the stories mirror each other: One is about a wild animal who tries to become human, and the other is about a boy who becomes a wild animal. Ten years later, the lives of Sendak and Silverstein would intersect again in a way that his fans might find very surprising.

that suppresses creativity and individual expression. Particularly contemptuous of those who mindlessly follow trends in fashion and slang, he criticized an early form of political correctness that he believed inhibited strong reactions to art, whether positive or negative. He also disapproved of the movement in children's literature to censor or gloss over all the unpleasant aspects of stories, most evident in the way fairy tales by the Brothers Grimm and others have been edited over the years.

Silverstein saw great hypocrisy in this trend, given the awful things children can see on the news every night. Fantasy violence is a natural, healthy outlet for children, he argued, and has a long, respectable tradition. Children understand the difference between fantasy violence and real life. If you forbid imaginary violence, however, and you overwhelm them with disturbing images from real life, you create an unhealthy situation in which children have no safe method to vent their anxieties. All of this explains quite a bit about Silverstein's taste for controversial subject matter and books that challenge children to think for themselves. It also cannily predicts the state of affairs today, where more and more children, at younger and younger ages, engage in acts of real violence.

The interviews also showed that Silverstein was something of a traditionalist when it came to his craft. In addition to his criticisms of the revision of timeless works, Silverstein also railed against postmodern artists and illustrators who refused to learn the basics of good draftsmanship. Instead, they tried to shortcut their way to fame with stylistic showmanship, the same way some of today's pop stars achieve fame based on their personas rather than any innate talent. Silverstein also showed great disdain for the trend in postmodern art that suggests it is the

Studs Terkel was a prominent Chicago radio personality when he first interviewed Shel Silverstein. During the interview, Silverstein opened up to Terkel more than he had to any member of the media. Terkel went on to become one of the most prolific interviewers in Chicago history.

responsibility of the reader, the viewer, or the audience to understand the artist's message. This is the idea that, if something fails, it is somehow the fault of the public and not the artist. Silverstein had no patience for such self-centered rationalization. It is important to share something with your audience, Silverstein argued, something they can readily understand and apply to their own lives. This gets to the core of his aesthetics, and it helps to explain his popularity.

A BUSY YEAR

1964 was a busy year for Silverstein. His new audience must have inspired him, because he published three more books in quick succession. First, however, he put together *Uncle Shelby's Zoo: Don't Bump the Glump! And Other Fantasies*. This book, which Silverstein dedicated to his sister Peggy, is a collection of drawings and short poems originally published in the December 1960 and February 1962 issues of *Playboy*. They depict a menagerie of imaginary animals reminiscent of Lewis Carroll's *Jabberwocky* or the fanciful creatures of Dr. Seuss. One notable surprise is Silverstein's use of watercolor. The bright colors evoke a world of pure fantasy, and the way the brushstrokes often stray outside the lines suggests a child's handiwork. Although not specifically intended for children, the poems that accompany these drawings also pave the way for his future collections in the way they consistently set up a concluding punch line or last-minute reversal. Unlike his other picture books, *Uncle Shelby's Zoo* has never been reissued; copies of it, if they can be found at all, are quite rare and valuable.

GIRAFFES AND RHINOS

Silverstein then wrote *A Giraffe and a Half*, the first of his titles that could truly be called a children's picture book. It has a simple rhyme scheme and a symmetrical structure. Each spread, or pair of pages, adds one silly aspect after another to the giraffe until the halfway point; then those same things are subtracted until we are left again with the original giraffe. The drawings mirror this progression, getting more dense and cluttered and then tapering off until we see just the boy and his giraffe again.

By the time he produced *A Giraffe and a Half,* Silverstein's artistic style had greatly matured. In *Lafcadio,* the lines were thin, and the drawings looked more like doodles. In *Giraffe,* the lines were thicker, which suggested a more confident hand. These thicker lines were mirrored in the choice of a bold typeface for the entire book, but the effect was somewhat awkward and amateurish. Nevertheless, Silverstein's use of space and the way he handled the book's overall layout are more sophisticated and deliberate.

There is no ambiguity in *A Giraffe and Half,* no moral to the story beyond perhaps the suggestion that things are best left alone, and animals and people alike should just be themselves. As in *Lafcadio,* the animal in the title is depicted almost exactly the same on the last page as he is on the first. Unlike the lion, however, the giraffe is apparently unchanged by the experience.

The same holds true for *Who Wants a Cheap Rhinoceros?*, another picture storybook published that same year. The target audience is a little older (the dust jacket says "ages 3–8"), so the humor is a little more mischievous. A few pages let Silverstein's subversive nature shine through, such as when he suggests the pet rhino could be used to collect "extra allowance from your father" or stop your mother from hitting you "when you haven't really done anything bad." Evidently, the version first published in 1964 had a little more mischief than the revised and expanded edition of 1983. In its current form, this is basically another book to be taken at face value: a simple catalog of all the surprising and funny uses for such a unique pet.

What makes *Rhinoceros* stand out from Silverstein's other books is the use of color on the cover. Some commentators think that these colors soften the feel of the book and make it more appealing to parents, particularly when it is paired with the loving image of a boy hugging a rhinoceros.[4] Silverstein was certainly aware of the fact that mothers and fathers buy books rather than children. He said as much in his radio interview with Studs Terkel. The colors in *Rhinoceros* could also simply be a holdover from his watercolor experiments in *Uncle Shelby's Zoo*. Silverstein would use color only once more in his career, on the cover of another book published in 1964, *The Giving Tree*. In the next chapter, we shall explore how the colors he chose, along with everything else in that book, has become the source of much debate.

This photograph of Shel Silverstein was taken in 1968, just four years after publication of perhaps his most well-known book, **The Giving Tree.** *The story of* **The Giving Tree** *seems simple on its face, but it has been interpreted and analyzed in many ways over the years since its publication.*

3

The Fabulist

IF *A GIRAFFE and a Half* and *Who Wants a Cheap Rhinoceros?* are simple picture books with no deep, hidden messages to be dug up or discussed, *The Giving Tree* is the exact opposite. In fact, it has generated more commentary and controversy than any other Silverstein book. Schoolteachers craft lesson plans around it, Christian ministers quote it in their sermons, and feminist scholars criticize its alleged support of female self-sacrifice. To date, it has sold more than 10 million copies and has been translated into 20 languages. Not bad for a book of approximately 500 words!

The story of *The Giving Tree* is deceptively simple. A tree and a boy form a tight friendship and engage in the simple pleasures of childhood play. The relationship between them is based on what the tree can offer the boy: leaves, shade, and a trunk to climb. In return, the tree receives only the boy's companionship and is satisfied to provide for him. As the boy grows up, however, he concerns himself more and more with worldly affairs (a girlfriend, money, a house); he leaves the tree all alone and only visits to take what he wants. The tree willingly sacrifices its apples, branches, and finally its trunk to serve the boy's needs, until nothing is left but a stump. In the end, the boy returns as a very old man who needs somewhere to sit. As always, the tree offers itself. "And the tree was happy," or so we are told, on the second-to-last page. We see a small picture of the old man sitting on the tree trunk and looking rather sad and lonely amidst all that white space.

The ambiguous nature of *The Giving Tree* has led to a wide range of interpretations. Is it a happy ending or not? Is Silverstein praising acts of selfless love and sacrifice, or condemning those selfish enough to take advantage of them? Does the boy represent humankind as a whole, men in particular, or just a typical boy? Does the tree represent Mother Nature, a human mother, some religious figure, or something else?

RELIGIOUS INTERPRETATIONS

The tree's selfless devotion to the boy, its willingness to sacrifice itself, and above all its bottomless well of forgiveness have led some Christian ministers to see the tree as a symbol for Jesus Christ. Many people find subtle support for this notion in the green and red colors used on the book's cover. Since these colors are most often associated with Christmas, and Silverstein hardly ever used color, they think there must be some significance.

In recent times, a rumor circulated that Silverstein had written the book in direct response to a conversation he had with a childhood friend who had since become a Jesuit priest. According to this story, the two men met in a park shortly after Silverstein had supposedly converted from Judaism to Christianity. The priest asked Silverstein to describe Jesus for him, and Silverstein delivered the book as his answer. This story turned out to be fabricated by the Jesuit minister himself, in support of sermons he was giving on the subject. By all accounts, Silverstein never participated in any organized religion and likely looked upon them with the same satirical eye he trained on everything else, yet religious scholars still find the book a worthy subject of debate.

OTHER READINGS

Some people see the tree as a bad example for children. According to this theory, since the tree does not limit its generosity and gives in to the boy's every whim, perhaps it teaches the boy to be selfish. A distinguished professor at Harvard has gone as far as to call the book "a nursery tale for the 'me' generation, a primer of narcissism, a catechism of exploitation."[1] As his friend Rik Elswit has attested, Silverstein was anything but selfish and, if anything, erred on the side of being too generous. It is therefore very unlikely that he wrote *The Giving Tree* in praise of selfishness.[2]

Others see the story as a parable of environmental destruction. In the beginning of the story, the boy does not hurt the tree when he uses its leaves, shade, and apples. It is only when he enters the real world that he decides to sell all of the tree's apples for money, instead of for his own enjoyment and sustenance, and to take all of the tree's branches for his house. It never occurs to him that, if he takes too much, he might destroy the tree and rob himself of a renewable resource. The same is often said of humankind and the way we have treated Mother Nature.

Feminists and other progressive thinkers make much of Silverstein's decision to portray the tree as a female. Such people see in the tree one of several variations on the theme of the exploited woman: a mother who sacrifices her own happiness for that of her child, a wife who does the same for her husband, or any woman too blinded by love to see that she wastes her life on a man who only uses her.

As was his custom, Silverstein refused to take sides or credit any of the broader interpretations of his book. Instead, he said in an interview for the *New York Times Book Review*, "It's just a relationship between two people; one gives and the other takes."[3]

In the same interview, Silverstein revealed a bit about his attitude toward happy endings and why so many of his books conclude with a more realistic dose of ambiguity: "Happy endings, magic solutions in children's books, [Silverstein] says, 'create an alienation' in the child who reads them. 'The child asks why I don't have this happiness thing you're telling me about, and comes to think when his joy stops that he has failed, that it won't come back.'"[4] When he forces children to think through an ambiguous ending, Silverstein not only teaches that real life is often both happy and sad, and that real people are seldom all good or all bad, he also equips them with the mental tools to create their own joy.

In another of those ironic twists so prevalent in Silverstein's career, it was precisely this ambiguity that initially

In 2004, Peter Frampton, who was a rock star in the 1970s, read to children at a public library in Cincinnati, Ohio. The book he chose was Shel Silverstein's **The Giving Tree.**

led publishers to reject the *The Giving Tree* as unsalable. William Cole, who was an editor at Simon & Schuster at the time, explains: "'Look Shel,' I said, 'the trouble with this *Giving Tree* of yours is that it falls between two stools;

it's not a kid's book—too sad, and it isn't for adults—too simple."[5] Cole was not alone in this opinion; many on the staff at HarperCollins felt the same way.

The middle ground between child and adult is where Silverstein is most comfortable, and his ability to cultivate that fertile soil is a large part of his genius. He speaks honestly to children and does not sugarcoat the hard truths or spoon-feed the answers; this gives them the room and the confidence to form their own ideas. At the same time, Silverstein jolts adult readers out of their fixed notions and forces them to reexamine the world from a child's point of view. A fortunate side effect, for both Silverstein and his publishers, is that this effectively doubles his target audience. Children read his books to feel grown up, and adults read his books to feel like kids again.

Upon publication of *The Giving Tree*, however, it looked like William Cole might be right. The first print run was small (7,000 copies[6]), and initial sales were sluggish.

Did you know...

No less than five editions of *The Giving Tree* have appeared over the years. These include the first edition, thirtieth- and fortieth-anniversary editions, a "Gift Edition" marketed at high school and college graduates that featured gold trim and a removable to/from sticker, and a "Special Holiday Edition" distinguished by a red book jacket. Undoubtedly, this is one tree that just keeps on giving!

Reviewers did not know what to make of the book and largely ignored it. In time, though, the book became popular through word of mouth. As Ursula Nordstrom put it, in what would become an often-repeated phrase, "the body twitched,"[7] and a book that seemed destined to be dead in the water came alive and took flight. *The Giving Tree* became a common gift item for college students and adults, particularly at Christmas time, which paved the way for later books like Dr. Seuss's *Oh, The Places You'll Go!*, marketed for children but with a large adult audience.

Sales of *The Giving Tree* steadily increased, year after year, until Silverstein found himself on the bestseller list, a position he would occupy, off and on, for the rest of his life. Although he continued to draw and write as always, he also used his newfound success as a springboard to explore one of his other passions: making music. As we shall see in the next chapter, Shel Silverstein's talent as a musician and lyricist has been woefully overlooked and underappreciated.

Shel Silverstein first came to Greenwich Village, a section of New York City, in 1961. At the time, Greenwich Village was something of an artists' community, and Silverstein fit in well. Above, a young woman walks with a guitar along a Greenwich Village street in April 1961.

4

The Songwriter

ASK YOUR PARENTS or grandparents who were the best songwriters of the 1960s and 1970s, and they may mention Bob Dylan, Paul Simon, or Joni Mitchell. Ask somebody else, and you will probably get a different answer. Ask enough people, and the list could grow into the hundreds. One name that you will probably never find on that list, however, is Shel Silverstein.

It is not because Silverstein does not deserve the recognition. After all, his songs were good enough to be performed by some of most well-respected singers of the era: Johnny Cash, Bob

Dylan, Emmylou Harris, Loretta Lynn, Jerry Lee Lewis, and Kris Kristofferson, to name only a few. The unfortunate truth is that Silverstein was cursed with a raspy set of pipes; Al Rickets, the entertainment editor at *Stars & Stripes*, once said Silverstein's voice sounded like it was "screened through a Brillo pad."[1] Silverstein was not embarrassed about it, though. "I don't see anyone running out and buying my records. But I like the way I sing."[2]

Although Silverstein was unashamed of his voice, he was smart enough to realize that his songs would reach a greater audience if he allowed other people to sing them. Some of his songs became signature hits and were forever associated with the performer. As a result, almost no one remembers that Shel Silverstein wrote them, and his talents as a songwriter remain largely unknown.

GATE OF HORN TO GREENWICH VILLAGE

As with his work on children's books, apparently it did not occur to Silverstein to write songs until someone else suggested it. Back in Chicago, following his military service and during his early tenure at *Playboy*, Silverstein began to haunt the Gate of Horn, a folk club established in 1956 by Albert Grossman, who would later become famous as the manager of Bob Dylan and Janis Joplin. Folk music was just beginning to be popular again, and one of the talents leading the revival was Bob Gibson, a frequent headliner at the Gate of Horn. Silverstein met and befriended Gibson and, according to Gibson's daughter, Meridian Green, it was Gibson who convinced the cartoonist to try his hand at songwriting. "But I'm not a songwriter," Silverstein responded. "Sure you are," said Gibson, "You just haven't done it yet."[3]

At the time, Silverstein lived at the Playboy Mansion, where he constantly rubbed elbows with celebrities and artists. The environment proved stimulating and, sure enough, he quickly discovered that songs flowed from his pen as fast as poems and illustrations. He soon had enough songs to land his own three-week engagement at the Gate of Horn.

It was with Bob Gibson that Silverstein first came to Greenwich Village in 1961. The pair lived together in a little studio apartment on Hudson Street, wrote songs, and generally immersed themselves in a community that was once again the epicenter of all that was hip and happening. Greenwich Village had long attracted unique artists, as far back as the early 1900s, due in large part to the establishment of art galleries, theaters, and publishing houses that supported their work. As beatniks like Jack Kerouac and Allen Ginsberg of the 1950s gave way to the folksters of the 1960s, a new generation of cultural icons took their place—people like Bob Dylan and Joan Baez. These singular personalities became lightning rods for like-minded bohemians eager to attend the next cultural revolution and, as a result, the Village continued its tradition as a hotbed of creativity.

At the time that Gibson and Silverstein moved to New York, Gibson had just released *Gibson and Camp at the Gate of Horn*, an influential record that captured a series of live performances from April of that year with Hamilton Camp, Gibson's former partner. In the audience during those sessions was 19-year-old Roger McGuinn, who later formed the Byrds, the biggest folk-rock band of all time; he credits Bob Gibson in general and those shows in particular as his primary inspiration.

Sadly, Bob Gibson was not able to enjoy the huge success of his peers. In the mid 1960s, he succumbed to a serious drug addiction and disappeared from the scene for a while. By the time he had cleaned up, folk music had become old news, and it was difficult for Gibson to find an audience. Nevertheless, Gibson and Silverstein remained close friends for the rest of their lives, and although he would collaborate with many other songwriters, Silverstein would always credit Gibson's influence as preeminent. At a party for Gibson, held just a week before Gibson's death in 1996, Silverstein said, "I don't just love Bob Gibson. I am Bob Gibson. Because what he was comes into me and it comes out in the other stuff that I do."[4]

FOLK SONGS

Silverstein had already released his *Hairy Jazz* album on Elektra Records, and Atlantic Records released another LP, *Inside Folk Songs,* in 1962. In the liner notes, William Cole, who was the Simon & Schuster editor who had passed on publishing *The Giving Tree,* jokingly struggles with an adequate description for Silverstein's voice. "Is he a tenor? Well, yes . . . and then again, no. Does he sound like a creaking door? A rusty gate? He does sound a little like he'd been chain-smoking for six straight weeks; but he doesn't smoke at all." Cole goes on to give the album genuine praise, however, for its musicianship, "sheer lunatic humor," and "acute insights into how people feel and react."[5]

The lyrics to *Inside Folk Songs* range from very adult ("Never Bite a Married Woman on the Thigh") to child-friendly. Both "Boa Constrictor" and "The Unicorn" would be published in almost exactly the same form 12 years later in *Where the Sidewalk Ends*. In the interim, a Canadian folk group called the Irish Rovers recorded "The Unicorn" for their 1967 album of the same name and turned it into a smash hit. It was Silverstein's first major success as a song-writer, but it would not be his last.

BRAGGER'S BLUES

In 1965, Silverstein recorded another album with the tongue-in-cheek title, *I'm So Good That I Don't Have to Brag.* This is a decidedly adult record, with hilariously risqué lyrics that are inappropriate for younger ears. It was recorded live, over two nights at a Chicago club called Mother Blues, and released under the Cadet imprint of Chess Records, a label that was almost exclusively devoted to recording African-American blues musicians. Although possibly fictional, the following interview included in its liner notes gives a good sense of Silverstein's attitude and strategy toward the media's attempt to pigeonhole him as an artist.

Q. How do you think your present image as world traveler, bawdy singer, etc. combines with your image as a writer of children's books?

A. I don't think about my image.

Q. But if you are a spokesman and leader of your generation with millions of followers, don't you care what they think?

A. I don't speak for anybody but me; I am not a leader. I just want them to let me alone so I can do my thing.

Q. What is your thing?

A. I don't know. That depends on the day, the time of day, and what I did yesterday.

Q. Do you admit that your songs and drawings have a certain amount of vulgarity in them?

A. No, but I hope they have a certain amount of realism in them.

Q. Do you shave your head for effect or to be different, or to strike back at the long-haired styles of today?

A. I don't explain my head.

Q. Why do you have a beard?

A. I don't have a beard. It's just the light; it plays funny tricks.

. . .

Q. You write poems and plays, you write songs and stories, and you draw cartoons and write children's books. People say you are a genius. Do you think you are a genius?

A. No, I think that I am just lucky.

Q. Are you being sarcastic again?

A. Just ask me an intelligent question.

Q. Do you believe the newspapers are out to get you?

A. No, but they occasionally do exaggerate.[6]

Silverstein's next album, *Drain My Brain*, was released the following year. Also from Cadet Records, it is another wide-ranging affair with numbers that swing from rocking ("Drain My Brain") to heartbreaking ("I Can't Reach the Sun"). In the liner notes, Herb Gardner concisely describes the experience of listening to a Shel Silverstein record:

Drop the needle anywhere and you will pick up a piece of Shel's mind. He is the best kind of artist because he reveals himself every time out and because it is Shel, this album will demand all of your attention. Shel, by actual count, is forty-seven people, and what you have got here is the original cast album.[7]

DOCK OF THE BAY

Ever ahead of the cultural curve, Silverstein headed out west around the time *Drain My Brain* was released and dropped into the nascent San Francisco scene. As he continued to bop about the country, he documented his travels for *Playboy* and left friends and lovers forever uncertain of his whereabouts. Northern California, like New York and Chicago before that, became a home base and favorite retreat. He bought a houseboat in Sausalito, located at the north end of the Golden Gate Bridge, and began to frequent local bars and cafes in search of like-minded musical accomplices. One such friend was a young guitarist named Rik Elswit, whom Silverstein would later help become a member of the group called Dr. Hook and the Medicine Show.

A COUNTRY BOY (NAMED SHEL)

In 1969, as everyone around him made rock albums, Silverstein shifted gears yet again and paid tribute to his love of country music with the release of his fifth album, *A Boy Named Sue and His Other Country Songs*. The rambling title song tells the first-person story of a man given the girl's name by his no-good father, who abandoned his wife and baby when the boy was only three. Everyone picks on and laughs at the boy, who grows up full of bitterness. Eventually, he heads off to find and kill his father. They finally meet in a bar and have a terrible fistfight, and the son pulls a gun on his father and is about to shoot him. When his father tells him he should be thankful for his name because it made him the man that he is, the son realizes his father is right, and the two men reconcile. The song ends in a typical Silverstein turnabout, as the son says that he would nevertheless name his own son anything but Sue.

Silverstein had been pitching songs to Chet Atkins, then vice president of RCA's country division and a noted musician in his own right, since the mid 1960s. Atkins is credited with helping to create what is now known as the

Nashville Sound, a more sophisticated and radio-friendly style of country music that appealed to a much larger audience. Silverstein explained it himself in a later interview:

> Now, country music and other kinds of music are getting together more. Rock people are picking up country, and country people are picking up rock rhythms. And people in the south aren't necessarily "country" fans anymore. The young ones are rock 'n roll fans. I know some people that are concerned about all the merging, but on the highest creative level, usually the really talented musical people love all good music if it's done well, you can appreciate c[ountry] & w[estern], or even a good polka. "Love this, hate that", that's usually the fan talking, not the musician.[8]

Ever on the cutting edge, Silverstein began to visit Nashville even before this country music revolution began, and there he met the Man in Black, Johnny Cash. As the story goes, Silverstein, Stephen Stills (of Crosby, Stills, and Nash), and Bob Dylan were all at Johnny Cash's house, where they played new songs for each other. Dylan debuted "Lay Lady Lay" (one of his better-known songs), Stills played "Suite: Judy Blue Eyes" (his best song), and Silverstein sang "A Boy Named Sue." Cash liked Silverstein's song so much that he later gave an impromptu performance of it at one of his most famous concerts, at the San Quentin prison. Cash read the lyrics from a page in front of him and the inmates erupted with laughter at all the right moments. An album was made from the recording of that concert, and Cash's live rendition of "A Boy Named Sue" became one of his all-time best-selling songs, shooting to number one on the country charts and number two on the pop charts. Cash was always careful to cite its true author, though, and of all the Silverstein songs that other artists recorded, "A

Boy Named Sue" remains the one that bears the unmistakable stamp of its creator.

TWO FIRSTS: FILMS AND FATHERHOOD

In 1970, Atlantic Records capitalized on the name Silverstein had made for himself with "A Boy Named Sue" and rereleased *Inside Folk Songs* under a new title, *Inside Shel Silverstein*. Never a big seller, the album nonetheless cemented Silverstein's reputation as a songwriter of note.

On June 30, 1970, Silverstein's first child, Shoshanna, was born. Her mother was a woman named Susan Hastings, with whom Silverstein had a relationship but did not marry. Unfortunately, next to nothing is known about Hastings or the extent to which Silverstein participated in Shoshanna's upbringing. An anecdote he shared with a journalist in 1978 does shed some light on his style of fathering, though. Shoshanna, age six in the story, was at his home in Key West when she lost a baby tooth. Like every other kid her age, she promptly placed it under her pillow, expecting to wake up with a quarter from the tooth fairy in its place. Shel Silverstein was not like most fathers, however, and did not want to perpetuate fairy tale lies. Duly disappointed, his daughter threw a tantrum. Silverstein relented when he realized that his parental honesty was causing more harm than good.[9]

Fatherhood was not the only new experience for Silverstein around that time. He branched out into yet another area of entertainment when he was hired to write the film score for *Ned Kelly*, a movie about the exploits of a famous Australian outlaw. The film was doomed from the start. In addition to an American songwriter, Rolling Stones frontman Mick Jagger (a Brit) was cast in the title role, and American singers Kris Kristofferson and Waylon Jennings were also involved in the project. Australians felt that natives should be used to tell such a particularly Australian story, and the amount of bad press this generated damaged the movie's reputation even before it hit the big screen.

Although *Ned Kelly* was unsuccessful, it paved the way for Silverstein to write another score for *Who Is Harry Kellerman and Why Is He Saying Those Terrible Things About Me?* the following year. Dustin Hoffman starred in this film about a day in the life of a hugely successful, but highly neurotic, songwriter. It was a defining moment for Silverstein; his old friend Herb Gardner wrote the screenplay, and Silverstein himself was given his first chance to act on the big screen, in the bit part of Bernie. Most important, the movie introduced Silverstein to a band that would soon become his main musical mouthpiece.

DR. HOOK AND THE MEDICINE SHOW

Silverstein and musical director Ron Haffkine, an old friend of Silverstein's from his folk music days, were searching for a relatively unknown band to perform his songs in *Who Is Harry Kellerman*. The manager for an upstart outfit that called themselves Dr. Hook and the Medicine Show played Haffkine some demo tapes of the band, which at the time was performing at dive bars in Union City, New Jersey. Haffkine loved what he heard, promptly signed on as their new manager, and played the tapes for Silverstein, who was equally enthusiastic.

Dr. Hook and the Medicine Show played every Silverstein tune on the soundtrack, including the film's theme song, "Last Morning." They also found themselves featured in the movie and onstage with Silverstein and Dustin Hoffman, during a segment when a live performance was shot at the legendary Fillmore East, a venue for many of the era's most memorable rock concerts. As a result, Dr. Hook

Silverstein wrote the score for the movie Who Is Harry Kellerman and Why Is He Saying Those Terrible Things About Me? *in 1971. The music was performed by what was at the time a relatively unknown band, Dr. Hook and the Medicine Show. After the movie, however, the band became quite successful. Above, they perform on stage in 1970.*

and the Medicine Show were immediately lifted out of obscurity and onto the national scene. An audition for CBS Records chief Clive Davis landed them a recording contract, and their career was off and running.

Silverstein wrote every song on their self-titled debut album, including the huge hit "Sylvia's Mother," which quickly shot to number one on the pop charts, both stateside and in Britain. In fact, this song about love thwarted by a girlfriend's meddling mother, was played in such heavy rotation that, by the end of the summer in 1972, even the band was tired of it. When they got ready to go on the road in support of the album, Silverstein nominated his friend, Sausalito guitarist Rik Elswit, as an excellent addition to the band. In a 1999 article for *Salon*, written just a few weeks after Silverstein's death, Elswit divulged that "Sylvia's Mother" was actually based on real events.[10] As it turns out, Silverstein had already admitted as much in a 1972 article for *Rolling Stone:*

> I just changed the last name, not to protect the innocent, but because it didn't fit. It happened about eight years ago and was pretty much the way it was in the song. I called Sylvia and her mother said, "She can't talk to you." I said, "Why not?" Her mother said she was packing and she was leaving to get married, which was a big surprise to me. The guy was in Mexico and he was a bullfighter and a painter. At the time I thought that was like being a combination brain surgeon and encyclopedia salesman. Her mother finally let me talk to her, but her last words were, "Shel, don't spoil it."[11]

Silverstein was not the type to get married anyway, and he ultimately left the real Sylvia alone. More interesting, though, than the biographical source for a hit song was Silverstein's apparent willingness to give away credits to his material. In the same article mentioned previously,

Did you know...

The unwitting extras in the scene from *Who Is Harry Kellerman* shot at the Fillmore East were actual concertgoers, there to see a Grateful Dead concert later that night. Director Ulu Grosbard wanted a live setting to give Dustin Hoffman's performance an air of realism.

Elswit cites several examples of Silverstein's creative generosity, such as when he offered two friends from his folksinging days equal credit on the song "Last Morning" simply because they gave him some passing advice on how to polish it up. They graciously declined, but Silverstein sincerely believed that art, particularly collaborative art, was not something you could break down into percentages. "You can't quantify magic," Elswit quotes him as saying, when the members of Dr. Hook argued over writing credits. "How can you possibly figure out what the most important parts of a song are? Art is magic and magic doesn't work like that."[12]

Silverstein continued his collaboration with Dr. Hook and the Medicine Show and wrote every song on their second album, called *Sloppy Seconds*. Among them was one titled "Cover of the Rolling Stone," which became the group's second single. This ironic bid for the attention of the premiere music magazine actually earned them the coveted cover spot in March 1973. It also embroiled the band in a bit of controversy in England, where the British Broadcasting Corporation (BBC) initially refused to play the song because they considered it free advertising for an American magazine. Eventually, a silly compromise was reached in which British DJs would yell "Radio Times" (the name of a British magazine) over the chorus. All of this only earned Dr. Hook and the Medicine Show more attention from the media, and sales of their records soared.

Unfortunately, Dr. Hook and the Medicine Show never managed to surpass their early successes, and their fame reached a plateau in the 1970s. Interpersonal differences and illness forced several personnel changes over the years, breaking down the band's cohesiveness. Silverstein continued to write songs for them, including the majority of their third album, and they had a few more hits, but when cofounder Ray Sawyer left the band in 1983 to pursue a solo career, it pretty much spelled the end. Nevertheless, in 15 years, they had earned eight gold records and legions of fans. Just recently, Dennis Locorriere, another original member, has revived the band's name and embarked on a greatest hits tour. No doubt, "Sylvia's Mother" and "Cover of the Rolling Stone" will expose a whole new generation to Silverstein's genius as a songwriter.

BOBBY BARE AND FRED KOLLER

During and directly following his tenure with Dr. Hook, Silverstein continued to collaborate with other musicians. One was country star Bobby Bare, whom Silverstein had met in 1970 through Chet Atkins. Bare and Silverstein had much in common, including a great appreciation for both country and folk music. At the time, Bare was about to switch record labels and Silverstein was occupied with Dr. Hook, but they met again three years later in Nashville, at an industry party at the house of songwriter Harlan Howard. Bare had just re-signed with RCA; he was tired of making records that were nothing more than vehicles to sell one or two hit singles, and he wanted to take his music in a new direction.

The notion of a concept album, with all the songs arranged around a common theme or narrative, had recently taken hold in rock music; the Beatles' *Sgt. Pepper's Lonely Hearts Club Band* popularized the form. Country music, however, had yet to adopt this trend. As Bare tells the story, he let Silverstein know that he wanted to make such a record on Saturday night at the party, and by that Monday morning, Silverstein called him from Chicago to say that the lyrics were finished. Silverstein flew back to Nashville, Bare loved what he heard, and he immediately booked some studio time. The result was *Lullabys, Legends and Lies*, arguably country's first concept album and the source of Bare's first number-one hit, "Marie Laveau."

Silverstein and Bare had so much fun that they made another record in 1975, titled *Bobby Bare and the Family Singin' in the Kitchen*. They produced more records, all the way up to 1998's *Old Dogs* (see Chapter 8), but none was as successful as their first.

Silverstein also formed a productive partnership during this period with folksinger Fred Koller. In 1973, Koller hitchhiked to Nashville with his Dobro guitar and immersed himself in the songwriter scene. A year later, he met Silverstein at one of the many haunts they both frequented, and the two formed a fast friendship based on their "mutual love for old bookstores, out of the way cafes, and [country music pioneer] Ernest Tubb."[13] The pair went on to write many songs together, some of which were recorded by other artists. Koller was a frequent guest of Silverstein's in Sausalito or on Martha's Vineyard until Silverstein's death in 1999, but the first album to really showcase their collaboration did not arrive until 2001, when Koller released *No Song Left to Sell* on Gadfly Records (see Chapter 8).

THE FREAKER'S BALL

Never one to give up on his own projects, Silverstein released two more original albums during this period: *Freakin' at the Freaker's Ball* (1972) and *Crouchin' on the Outside* (1973). The first was a satirical take on hippie culture, likely influenced in equal parts by his residence in swinging San Francisco and his rip-roaring times with Dr. Hook and the Medicine Show. The band returned the favor when it accompanied Silverstein on the album. Songs such as "Don't Give a Dose to the One You Love the Most," later sung by Dr. Hook for an anti-venereal disease campaign, and "I Got Stoned and I Missed It" reveal a seedier side to the children's author that few parents would be happy with, but, as always, Silverstein mixed things up. The one single that earned any radio play at all was a rendition of what would become his trademark children's poem, "Sarah Cynthia Sylvia Stout Would Not Take the Garbage Out." Likewise, the song "Peace Proposal" was published in poem form as "The Generals." Both were featured in *Where the Sidewalk Ends*.

Crouchin' on the Outside was a double-record reissue of two previous albums. The first two sides contained *I'm So Good That I Don't Have to Brag*, and the last two sides reprised *Drain My Brain*. The cover shot shows Silverstein in his trademark denim, beard, and bald head, looking fearsome enough to give little kids nightmares.

In November 1972, during work on his own albums, Silverstein contributed two songs to *Free to Be . . . You and Me*. The project, put together by actress Marlo Thomas, was first released as a children's album and illustrated songbook, and was later produced as a television special in 1974. Others involved included such entertainment luminaries as Harry Belafonte, Mel Brooks, Kris Kristofferson, Alan Alda, and a young Michael Jackson. Tom Smothers, of the Smothers Brothers, performed Silverstein's song, "Helping." Another track called "Ladies First," performed by Marlo Thomas, was based on a poem of the same name, which appeared 10 years later in *A Light in the Attic*. The aim of the project was to teach children the importance of diversity, tolerance, and self-esteem. *Free to Be . . . You and Me* has become something of a cultural touchstone for many who grew up during that era; it remains in print today, having sold more than 500,000 copies.

FAMILY LOSSES

On December 11, 1972, Silverstein's father, Nathan, died. Just three years later, on June 29, 1975, Shoshanna's mother, Susan Hastings, also died, of unknown causes. Shoshanna moved to Baltimore and thereafter was raised by her aunt and uncle, Curt and Meg Marshall. Both deaths seem to have softened Silverstein a bit, which can be seen in the preface to *Uncle Shelby's ABZ Book*. This marks the starting point in Silverstein's transition from the cynical and occasionally mean-spirited "Uncle Shelby," who had yet to be "blessed with children of his own," to the caring father figure who invites children to dream in *Where the Sidewalk Ends*.

> Many of my little friends have asked Old Uncle Shelby why he has written this book and why he loves children so dearly, and to these I must answer that although Uncle Shelby has never been blessed with children of his own, the little ones have always had a very special place in his tired old heart.
>
> Yes, I have heard them crying late at night, and I have thought about them—I have heard them playing and laughing outside my window while I was trying to sleep and I have thought about them—I have seen the pictures they have drawn on my car and I have thought and thought and thought about them. And so this book—to help all my little friends get all the things in life that they so richly deserve.[14]

Much had changed in the intervening 13 years. Silverstein had become a father, for one, while losing his own. He was also wildly successful in multiple creative outlets. As we will see in the next chapter, though, it was in his illustrated volumes of poetry that he found his true calling, as well as the medium where his fame would forever be assured.

Silverstein stands on a New York City street in 1973. The next year, his first collection of poetry for children, Where the Sidewalk Ends, *was published to wide acclaim.*

5

The Poet-Illustrator

THERE IS A story hidden within the subtitle to *Where the Sidewalk Ends*, and only Silverstein knows all the details. Perhaps Ursula Nordstrom, to whom the book was dedicated, could tell a part of it, if she were still alive. Silverstein alone knew the whole tale and, to our great misfortune, he is not with us anymore either.

What is so mysterious about the subtitle "the poems & drawings of Shel Silverstein"? To those of us who were raised on his books, Silverstein's illustrations are inseparable from his words. Sometimes they simply visualize for us a crazy idea in the poem. Sometimes they focus our attention on something we might otherwise overlook, and sometimes they just tell us a funny joke. The illustrations always serve some purpose, and they enrich the way we read Silverstein's work in ways we might not always be able to explain.

Silverstein considered himself a cartoonist, first and foremost; this is where he found his earliest inspiration and first professional work. We know that he was proud of his art. Whether or not he was serious, at one point he even referred to himself as the "finest line artist in America."[1] What then are we to make of the letter to Silverstein in *Dear Genius*, a book of Ursula Nordstrom's correspondence, in which his stalwart editor casually offers her support for Silverstein's request that someone else illustrate *Where the Sidewalk Ends*? Specifically Maurice Sendak?[2] It is the only letter to Silverstein included in the collection, so clearly this detail is meant to surprise and intrigue us. Was Silverstein having a crisis of confidence? Was he still smarting from Jean Shepherd's playful barb that he was "not for children, of whatever age"?

We know that Silverstein was generous with his talent and quite literally liked to spread the wealth. According to Rik Elswit, if somebody was even in the room with him as he wrote a song, they were likely to get a writing credit and whatever financial reward that entailed.[3] Did Silverstein intend to offer Sendak a chance to achieve the same kind of success and exposure he had reached 10 years earlier with *Where the Wild Things Are*?

This is probably not the case. Sendak was still a leading children's author, who had just recently been awarded a Hans Christian Andersen medal for illustration, the only American to ever receive such an honor. It is much more likely that Silverstein simply felt a kinship with Sendak and trusted him to capture the spirit of his poems. In the letter mentioned previously, Nordstrom refers to a "long ago" meeting between the two author/illustrators, during which they developed genuine affection and respect for one another.[4] This respect was no doubt reaffirmed in 1970 when Silverstein read Sendak's latest book, *In the Night Kitchen*. The tone of this dreamlike story about a boy who gallivants naked around a bakery bears more than a passing affinity to Silverstein's work. The idea of a collaboration between two of the greatest living talents in children's literature must have been compelling indeed.

Nordstrom's reference in another letter in *Dear Genius* to "thousands of pieces of paper and . . . millions of changes" tells us that *Sidewalk* was an editorial nightmare, and that Silverstein changed his mind often.[5] Perhaps this idea of an outside illustrator was merely a passing notion, but the fact that it was suggested at all, let alone supported by his otherwise impeccable editor, is still quite shocking.

If Silverstein were alive today and able to read these words, he would likely say that there is no story in that

Did you know...

Where the Sidewalk Ends and *In the Night Kitchen* have both been consistently banned from many libraries throughout America. Some people think a few of the illustrations in both books, as well as the rebellious content of some of Silverstein's poems, are not appropriate for children.

Silverstein apparently had qualms about illustrating his book
Where the Sidewalk Ends, *and his editor, Ursula Nordstrom,*
apparently suggested that another famous artist and author for
children, Maurice Sendak, draw the illustrations. Sendak is shown
above checking his art at home in 1988.

subtitle. It simply describes what is in the book—no more and no less. He would also want his readers to develop their own ideas and interpretations; to this reader, the story that subtitle tells is one of an artist who finds his true calling. During the creation of *Where the Sidewalk Ends*, Silverstein realized that the real magic in his work was in the marriage of his words with his drawings and, to the great delight of children everywhere, he decided to illustrate the book himself after all.

OF DREAMS AND MAGIC

The first few pages of *Sidewalk* are filled with references to magic and the powers of the imagination. The title page is adorned with an illustration of two heads that wear masks. Students of drama might see in these large-nosed disguises an echo of the comedy and tragedy symbols of the theater. Even if this is unintentional, Silverstein obviously references the act of make-believe. The opening poem is, after all, an "Invitation" to dreamers, pretenders, and magic bean buyers.

The second poem, "Acrobats," evokes the magic of the circus and, in its last line, warns that to enter the world of dreams and magic is a delicate high-wire act that can all be destroyed with little more than a sneeze. The drawing on the dedication page emphasizes this fragility. What is more evocative of childhood wonder than a little hand that holds a balloon? The dart-shaped bird on the facing page suggests an impending pop. The fourth poem, "Homemade Boat," is also cautionary; it shows how disastrous it can be if you do not design your dreams with the real world in mind.

The third poem in the book brings us back to where this chapter began. "Magic" tells of all the fantastical creatures encountered by friends, but ends with the telltale line "But all the magic I have known / I've had to make myself." The absence of any illustration emphasizes Silverstein's message, and forces the reader to imagine one of his or her own. This little gem of a poem would have been vastly different with a detailed drawing of ghosts and goblins by Maurice Sendak—or anyone else, for that matter.

ODDBALLS AND BAD HABITS

Many of Silverstein's best-known poems are tall tales about strange children or adults whose bad habits bring down outrageous forms of ruin upon them. Poems such as "Jimmy Jet and His TV Set," "Sarah Cynthia Sylvia Stout Would Not Take the Garbage Out," and "The Dirtiest Man" are often included in children's poetry anthologies; they are chosen because they are characteristic examples of his work, but perhaps even more because these poems are the closest Silverstein comes to the kind of cautionary sermon that some feel should be a central theme of children's literature. As commentator Ruth MacDonald points out, however, the situations in this poems are too ridiculous, too funny, and ultimately too unrealistic to be applicable in the real world.[6]

Moreover, Silverstein balances these cautionary tales with others poems about similarly strange individuals in which he either passes no judgment at all, or else seems to celebrate oddness for its own sake. Who could read "Ickle Me, Pickle Me, Tickle Me Too" and not share in the excitement of their reckless ride into the wild blue yonder, or not appreciate the smug satisfaction of Melinda Mae when she finally finishes eating her whale, just "because she said she would"? Surely we are meant to sympathize with "Hector the Collector" and "The Long-Haired Boy"

A young boy recites a Silverstein poem at a celebration of the author's work in 2005. Where the Sidewalk Ends *is still widely read by children today.*

and not those "sightless people" who ostracized them because they were different.

Elsewhere in *Sidewalk*, so-called bad habits are positively celebrated. "My Hobby" delights in how much fun it is to spit on people's heads from atop tall buildings; "Stone Telling" suggests people throw stones at windows; "Rudy Felsh" admires the art of burping; and "Thumbs" gives tacit support to those who suck on them too much. All readers of Silverstein, even the young ones, realize what an impish trickster he is, and so his mischievous advice is always taken with a grain of salt. "Ma and God" is considerably more subversive, as Silverstein usurps a mother's power to enforce her rules by opposing them with our divine birthrights. For every admonition ("Don't splash," "Use your fork"), Silverstein gives us a God-given reason to ignore it, and what mother can win an argument with God?

Should there be any doubt remaining about whether Silverstein intended any of his work to limit the scope of acceptable kid behavior, we need only read "Listen to the Mustn'ts." In eight short lines, Silverstein subverts the entirety of parental authority: "Anything can happen, child, ANYTHING can be." The same theme runs through "My Rules," only in reverse. Put too many conditions on those you love, or more specifically those who you want to love you, and you just may find yourself alone.

MORE VIEWS FROM THE DUGOUT

When he is not championing the power of the imagination or challenging authority, Silverstein often offers us a chance to look at the world from the viewpoint of the underdog or the outsider. Sometimes this means giving voice to the simple but often marginalized joys and sorrows of being a child (see "Tree House" and "What a Day"). He is much more effective and unique, however, when he flips the world upside-down, such as when he considers the fate of what gets eaten in poems like "Early Bird" and "Point of View," or when he inverts a familiar phrase and creates one of his own, as in the charming poem "Hug O' War."

Given the pervasive assumption that human beings are competitive and warring by nature, Silverstein's idealistic wish for a world in which "everyone wins" is more radical than it seems. It also reveals his bohemian leanings. Further hints at a hippie behind the wheel are found in "Colors," his subtle attack on racism; "My Beard," with its silly drawing of the naked hairy man on the run; and "The Generals," his not-so-subtle satire on war.

Upon its publication in 1974, *Where the Sidewalk Ends* became an instant classic. It quickly skyrocketed to the top of the bestseller list and earned an Outstanding Book Award from the *New York Times*. Nearly 5 million copies have been sold in the years since, making it the all-time best-selling book of children's poetry. Never again would Silverstein have to wonder whether he was the right man for the job.

Parents and children gather to listen to readings of Shel Silverstein's poems at Poet House in New York City on April 30, 2005. Though Silverstein died in 1999, his work continues to be very popular.

6

The Shapeshifter

AFTER THE PUBLICATION of *Where the Sidewalk Ends*, Silverstein returned to the allegory picture-book format with *The Missing Piece*. Published in 1976 (and reprinted in a thirtieth-anniversary edition in 2006), this deceptively simple story of a Pacman-shaped character in search of its completing segment is an example of Silverstein the minimalist. The drawings are little more than shapes and lines, and each page contains one or two sentences at most.

The plot concerns the character's trials and tribulations along its quest for fulfillment, as it travels through rain and snowstorms, meets pieces that do not quite fit (or do not want to), and stops to smell flowers or talk to worms. When it finally does find a piece that fits, the experience is not as perfect as anticipated. It discovers that it is harder to sing properly because its mouth is filled by the piece, and it rolls too fast to pause and appreciate the simple pleasures in life. "I could have ended the book there," Silverstein later said in an interview. "But instead it goes off singing: it's still looking for the missing piece. That's the madness of the book, the disturbing part of it."[1] In the end, the shape abandons its matching piece and rolls away.

As in *The Giving Tree*, Silverstein instills this bittersweet story with subtle insights on human relationships. Essentially, he refutes the traditional wisdom that we can only be complete when paired with another. Often, it is the search and not the discovery that proves most fulfilling in life. Often, the object of our affection is not everything we hope it will be. Often, those very same things that provide comfort and security can also hold us back and hamper self-expression. All these ideas and more are implied in *The Missing Piece*, but as always Silverstein expresses them in a relatively ambiguous manner that allows room for dissention or agreement among his readers.

Five years after the release of *The Missing Piece*, Silverstein produced a sequel called *The Missing Piece Meets the Big O*. This story gives the missing piece center stage and narrates its reciprocal search for a soul mate. This time, however, the searcher is passive. The missing piece is not round and so it cannot roll; it must instead wait for whatever happens to come along. That is really the key difference between the two books: The first examines the nature of fulfillment, while the second explores the individual's role in and responsibility to achieve that fulfillment. After the missing piece encounters all sorts of literal misfits and attempts various methods to make itself more attractive, the piece finally meets what appears to be its perfect match.

As in the first book, this union is not a happy end to the quest, but rather a bittersweet epiphany. In the sequel, the missing piece begins to grow, while its mate stays the same shape. As a result, they no longer fit together and are forced to part. Saddened by its loss, the missing piece then encounters another shape called the Big O. A complete circle, the Big O needs no additional pieces. Instead, it teaches the missing piece how to wear off its sharp corners and roll on its own. When the story ends, the missing piece is fully rounded and rolls off with the Big O.

Intentionally or not, Silverstein reveals in these two books quite a bit about his own philosophy of love and commitment. Although both stories leave room for argument about the ultimate lessons learned by the shapes and whether those lessons apply to everyone, Silverstein is clearly calling into question the idea that there is a perfect match for everyone. Quite simply, Silverstein does not seem to buy it. Moreover, he suggests that such an expectation can only end in compromise or disappointment. He did not believe in marriage or monogamy in his own life, and although few children will be savvy enough to glean that attitude themselves, it will not be lost on their parents. Uncle Shelby, it seems, was not only alive and well, but continuing to sneak his way into Silverstein's books for children.

ENLIGHTENED VERSE

In 1981, between the release of *The Missing Piece* and its sequel, Shel Silverstein produced what many consider to be his crowning achievement. *A Light in the Attic* was different from *Where the Sidewalk Ends* in a number of ways. There were no crises of confidence preceding its creation and no question that Silverstein would be the sole author and illustrator. Nothing suggests the kind of belabored editing process that plagued *Sidewalk*. First and foremost, it was designed and written as a single volume, not cobbled together from old songs and scraps of other publications. Consequently, it has a unity of form and vision that the first book lacks. Moreover, Silverstein displays a heightened consciousness of his readership that may be attributed to having a daughter in the same age range. He even dedicates *Attic* to "Shanna" (Shoshanna), who turned 11 the year it was published. In addition, the dedication page has a drawing of a flower, and *Shoshanna* means "rose" in Hebrew. As Ruth MacDonald puts its, "the book has a clearer sense than does *Sidewalk* of its audience and the length of its narrative and better expresses children's interests, needs, and unspoken fears and desires."[2]

MacDonald also points out that *Attic* appears to be have been targeted at a more mature audience than *Sidewalk*.

> There is more focus on school and schoolwork, more clever, artful dodging of adult prohibitions, and more wordplay. The several voices that Silverstein assumes as a poet are more coaxing and teasing, as if the child were more reticent and had more complex skills with which to avoid adults than the younger, more easily engaged child assumed in *Sidewalk*.[3]

DIVING IN

Attic and *Sidewalk* still have quite a bit in common, though. On the surface, they share a classical structure. Both begin with poems that address readers directly and welcome them into Silverstein's world. As in many traditional collections of verse, these inaugural poems also serve as invocations;

they call on the muse of imagination to create a magical place that both poet and reader can inhabit and commune in for a time. Both books also conclude with poems that challenge readers to set off on their own imaginative journeys.

Sidewalk ends with "The Search," a poem that suggests that the fabled pot of gold at the end of the rainbow is not an end but rather the beginning of another quest. In *A Light in the Attic*, "This Bridge" only spans halfway across the gulf between reality and fantasy, boredom and adventure, and leaves it up to the reader to build the other half. A drawing that accompanies the poem shows a childlike figure that stands where the unfinished bridge ends and looks down into space.

The idea of a child alone at the edge of the unknown is a recurring motif in Silverstein's work, easily traced through a series of similar poems and drawings in *Where the Sidewalk Ends*. First, there is the cover illustration, which does not actually accompany the title poem, but accompanies another one called "The Edge of the World." Then, there is the drawing of a boy forced to walk the plank by "Pirate Captain Jim." Lastly, we have "For Sale," which depicts a crying little girl who sits on the lip of a long auction block.

In all these poems, a child either literally or figuratively faces a drop into a void of blank white space. To varying degrees, all the drawings mentioned above evoke (as Mac-Donald suggests of "The Bridge"[4]) a rite of passage that many children share: the first leap from a diving board that so often marks the line between child and adolescent. Silverstein makes the analogy explicit in *Attic* with "Fancy Dive," a poem in which a high-diver's worst fear is realized when she discovers, on her way down, that "the pool had no water." In the accompanying illustration, another child sits poolside, a spectator with a rather smug look on her face that is familiar to anyone who has been publicly embarrassed.

EVERY BODY

A child who stands alone on the edge of a diving board for the very first time may have many fears beyond the possibility that he or she might get hurt. Following through on the leap may not be the hardest part. The anxiety of exposure—to bare oneself literally and figuratively to a crowd of onlookers—is the truly intimidating part. It is a cruel irony that children's bodies change in odd and unsettling ways at the exact same time that self-awareness becomes most acute.

Silverstein was no stranger to the awkwardness that attends the onset of puberty, and he admitted on several occasions that he felt like an outsider as a child. It is not surprising, then, that anxiety about body image pops up everywhere in his poems and drawings. *Where the Sidewalk Ends* features numerous poems in which physical changes are exaggerated for comic effect. Necks and noses are elongated and sliced off, whole bodies are eaten piece by piece, but Silverstein reserves particularly grotesque fates for the head, the most iconic body part of all. In "Us," "The Planet of Mars," and "The Loser," heads are doubled, moved, and removed entirely.

A Light in the Attic approaches this theme from the dual vantage point of a child who goes through adolescence and a man (Silverstein) who hits middle age. From the familiar nightmare that one has forgotten to wear pants in "Something Missing" to the ghoulish metamorphoses featured in "Headache," "Thumb Face," and "Skin Stealer," his poems and drawings tap into the estrangement and helplessness we sometimes feel toward our own bodies, particularly

during stages of change. Those changes are most pro-
nounced when we are very young and very old, a fact Silverstein explicitly confronts in "The Little Boy and the Old
Man," in which the title characters reveal an identical set
of physical and emotional sensitivities to the incidents that
take place in their daily lives, such as dropping their spoons
or wetting their pants.

OTHER STRESSORS

Adolescents worry about a lot more than their own bodies, though, and Silverstein covers the gamut of concerns.
"The Little Boy and the Old Man" not only draws parallels
between the physical frailties of the old man and the little
boy, it also exposes the emotional isolation they both feel
when ignored by adults. "Rockabye," in which an older sibling puts a baby up in a tree, directly precedes that poem, on
the facing page. This poem hints at the jealousy a child can
feel upon the arrival of a new sibling, without ever explicitly stating how the baby got there. Silverstein based the
wording and cadence on the familiar lullaby, which helps
evoke the confusing mixture of love and resentment the
child feels—the alternating desire to protect and repel.

Simpler yet no less nagging stressors like schoolwork,
doctor visits, babysitters, and household chores are tackled
in "The Homework Machine," "Examination," "Sitter,"
and "Messy Room," respectively. The two poems that get
right to the core of childhood anxiety are "Nobody" and
"Whatif." Both poems expertly capture many of the negative thoughts that often trouble children, but they differ in
their approach. "Whatif" simply commiserates with all those
kids that worry and cannot sleep, but "Nobody" exposes the
source of those worries as nothing more than a figment of
one's imagination.

In this way, the "light in the attic" is not only a metaphor for the imagination, but a literal illumination that banishes the phantoms and makes the frightful feel familiar again.

A LITTLE RELIEF

Elsewhere, *A Light in the Attic* offers additional relief from the stresses of adolescence, both comic and advisory. The sheer silliness of "They've Put a Brassiere on the Camel" could help diffuse the drama that surrounds a first bra. "Little Abigail and the Beautiful Pony" provides a healthy outlet for the revenge fantasies concocted by every child denied something by his or her parents, and "Prayer of the Selfish Child" speaks to all those unspeakable thoughts we cannot, and probably should not, share with anyone. "How Not to Have to Dry the Dishes" goes so far as to suggest a destructive strategy to avoid that common chore.

Sometimes, though, crude humor is enough. Uncle Shelby is certainly not above bad puns, bare behinds, and funny little men whose ridiculously long beards hide their naked bodies. Nearly identical illustrations accompany the indexes in both *Sidewalk* and *Attic*.

Did you know...

A Light in the Attic is number 22 on the list of the 50 all-time best-selling children's books. Amazingly, Silverstein has two more books on the list as well: *Where the Sidewalk Ends* is number 12, and *The Giving Tree* is number 14.

Most subversive, though, are those poems in which Silverstein seems to speak directly to his reader and offers advice from the heart. Both "Tryin' on Clothes" and "Outside or Underneath" suggest that it is the most natural thing in the world to be naked, and that nothing you wear will ever really matter. Neither poem is written for comic effect, or to shock. Silverstein knows that the fixation on clothes and other material goods begins early in our society, and he simply offers a dissenting opinion.

SALES AND CRITICAL REACTION

The kinds of poems discussed above tackle subjects that are awkward at best, and outright taboo in the minds of some parents; as a result, they are also the ones that seem to get Silverstein into the most trouble. It has never been tolerated in America to depict nudity or disobedience in books for children, let alone to advocate them, but this feeling was even stronger during the conservative 1980s, when *A Light in the Attic* was published. As a result, this book, like *Sidewalk* before it, came under fire from several parent groups, who succeeded in getting it banned at many local and school libraries. To this day, *A Light in the Attic* remains on the American Library Association's list of the 100 Most Frequently Challenged Books.

The backlash did little to stem sales of the book; if anything, the book likely gained even greater fame because of it. *A Light in the Attic* hit the *New York Times* bestseller list right out of the gate and stayed there for a record 182 weeks. The *School Library Journal* gave it a Best Book Award, and numerous other prizes soon followed. Shel Silverstein had become a certified phenomenon and a millionaire in the process.

Silverstein bought a house in Key West, Florida, which became one of his primary retreats during the winter months. Above is a scenic view of boats docked in a marina in Key West.

Different Dances

BY THE LATE 1970s, Shel Silverstein's creative energy was exploding in all directions. When *A Light in the Attic* was published in 1981, he had become the undisputed king of children's poetry. Nevertheless, Silverstein continued adventuring in other realms. In 1977, he contributed to another original motion picture score, for the film *Thieves*. Starring Marlo Thomas and Charles Grodin, this comedy about love and reconciliation was based on a play by Silverstein's friend Herb Gardner, who also wrote the screenplay.

After *Thieves*, Silverstein produced *Songs & Stories,* in 1978, which follows in the same vein as *Freakin' at the Freaker's*

Ball. It takes satirical and irreverent potshots at everything from the drug culture ("The Smoke Off," "They Held Me Down") to interspecies romance ("The Cat and the Rat"). The musical content, however, is more akin to *Inside Folk Songs*. Silverstein accompanies himself on acoustic guitar, and he dusts off and reinterprets "Never Bite a Married Woman on the Thigh," which originally appeared on *Inside Folk Songs*, for *Songs & Stories*.

The following year, 1979, brought a second album, *The Great Conch Train Robbery*. Backed by an all-star band of country and western musicians, Silverstein entertained his inner outlaw with songs about bad men and the women who loved and sometimes left them. The title track recounts one of Silverstein's trademark tall tales, about a shrimper (or shrimp boat fisherman) named Sam, who tires of his work-a-day life and decides to rob the Conch Train, which takes wealthy tourists on a tour around Key West, Florida. Since this is a Shel Silverstein song, the heist ends badly. A tourist sharpshooter guns down old Sam and ends his robber days before they even begin.

Conch is a local slang term that originally applied to immigrants from the Bahamas who settled in Key West, but it eventually came to mean anyone who lived there long term. The island had become another favorite retreat of Silverstein's, primarily during the winter months. Silverstein eventually bought and restored a Greek revival house and writing studio on Williams Street in Key West, and it was there that he drew his final breath some 30 years later. Key West's perpetual sunshine, colorful locals, and a laid-back, tolerant lifestyle have always attracted artists and writers, from Ernest Hemingway and Wallace Stevens to Tennessee Williams.

Silverstein mentions Tennessee Williams by name in his song. Also, Sloppy Joe's bar, where Sam plans his robbery, was not only named after one of Hemingway's fishing buddies, but it was actually the site of a notorious fistfight between Hemingway and, you guessed it, Wallace Stevens.

Different Dances was also published in 1979. This oversized, coffee-table compendium of Silverstein's adult cartoons included many that had first appeared in *Playboy*. Jacket copy describes it this way: "Startling, irreverent and provocative, the incomparable creator of poems and fables for children now turns his eye and pen upon the social calamities and absurdities of the adult world." Although a twenty-fifth-anniversary edition was released in 2004 (in a smaller, abridged format), first-edition copies of the original now sell for several hundred dollars.

THE LADY OR THE TIGER

In 1981, Silverstein embarked on yet another career path when he wrote a one-act play called *The Lady or the Tiger Show*. Silverstein updated a famous short story by Frank Stockton about a medieval kingdom in which accused criminals are forced to choose their own fate. Behind one door awaits certain death; behind the other door is a beautiful woman. To make the story more modern, Silverstein created the character of a television producer who uses the format on a game show to boost his ratings. It is interesting to note that, at the same time, Stephen King was busy writing *The Running Man*, a novella that also concerns a do-or-die game show. (It was written under the pseudonym Richard Bachman and later made into a film starring Arnold Schwarzenegger.)

The Lady or the Tiger Show was first staged in New York City at the Ensemble Studio Theater's Marathon festival of one-act plays, and it starred Richard Dreyfuss in the lead role. The play was a minor hit and marked the emergence of Silverstein as a playwright to watch. Indeed, as the 1980s began, it seemed as if he could do no wrong. Everything he touched was a success. *A Light in the Attic* was a bestseller and had earned critical accolades, *Where the Sidewalk Ends* had recently been given the Michigan Young Readers' Award, and *The Missing Piece Meets the Big O* earned its writer an International Reading Association's Children's Choice Award.

Just as Silverstein's professional career reached its high point, his personal life took a turn for the worse. On April 24, 1982, his daughter, Shoshanna, died suddenly of a brain aneurysm in Baltimore. She was only 11 years old. Although Silverstein did not have a conventional relationship with his daughter, he nevertheless loved her very deeply. Shoshanna's death left him inconsolable. Hugh Hefner was quoted as saying, "It was the single most devastating event of his life, and he never really did recover from it."[1]

PLAYWRITING

As Silverstein tried to overcome his grief, he devoted a good part of the next two decades to his plays. In 1983, his group of one-act plays, collectively titled *Wild Life* (including *I'm Good to My Doggies*, *Chicken Suit Optional*, and *The Lady or The Tiger Show*) debuted off-Broadway to rave reviews. That same year, he wrote another one-act play called *Gorilla*. It was first staged at the Goodman Theater in Chicago; also on the bill that night was a play by fellow Chicago native David Mamet.

Although Mamet was 10 years younger than Silverstein, he was the more accomplished playwright, having already

David Mamet poses with his wife, Rebecca Pidgeon, in 1991. Silver-stein's play Gorilla *premiered at the same time that one of Mamet's plays was first staged in 1983, and the two became fast friends.*

written for film and television, as well as a couple of criti-cally acclaimed off-Broadway dramas. (The following year, Mamet would win both the Pulitzer Prize and a Tony Award for *Glengarry Glen Ross*, later made into a film of the same name.) Despite his own success, Mamet was starstruck when he met Silverstein. "Where I come from, Shel Silverstein was a demigod,"[2] he would later say. Mamet and Silverstein formed a fast friendship. Mamet and his wife (actress and singer Rebecca Pidgeon) even spent much of their honey-moon with Silverstein on Martha's Vineyard. Mamet later reflected, "I loved him. My family loved him. We all felt that being with him was an unexampled privilege."[3]

Silverstein bought a literal gingerbread house on Mar-tha's Vineyard, in the town of Oak Bluffs. This became one of his four primary hideaways; he also had the house-boat in Sausalito, the apartment in Greenwich Village, and the house in Key West. Clearly, he found the seaside very appealing, but ultimately it was the lifestyle and the other residents of those locales that really attracted him. All four places are populated by all kinds of artists and celebrities. As a result, locals have grown accustomed to seeing strange and famous people. Even if fans still seek out autographs, they generally manage to excercise restraint. Silverstein may have been a private person, but he was no recluse. Once he felt comfortable in a town, he could stay out all night, alone or otherwise. Many people have spotted Silverstein out on the street somewhere, late at night, as he poured his indomitable spirit into the ears of some willing listener. Although he shied away from the media, he always made time for his fans. Mamet described it this way:

> While we sat, every day, fans would find him out. Every day, women would come with their children, and their arms full of books. Not one book, but 10. And they would, sheepishly, ask him to inscribe the books. And Shel would say, of each one, "Who is this for?"" The woman would tell him a name, and Shel would fashion the name into an animal and inscribe the book to the kid.
>
> I'd sit by, watching him. And I never saw him hesitant, or put-upon, or at all reluctant. I asked him, "Shel, don't you ever find it an imposition?" And he smiled and said, "Are you kidding?"[4]

After *Gorilla,* Silverstein produced *Remember Crazy Zelda?* in 1984. Eight more plays followed over 1985 and 1986. Another play, called *Feeding the Baby*, was featured in an assembly of sketches by all-star playwrights, staged at

Lincoln Center under the title *Urban Blight* in 1988. They were all short, one-act affairs, and many were debuted at the Ensemble Theater's Marathon festival. They are certainly worthy of more attention and study than the present book allows—of all Silverstein's works, the plays have been the most overlooked.

THE GREATEST PRIZE

Silverstein did more than write plays. In 1983, he also "recited, sung and shouted" poems from *Where the Sidewalk Ends* for a Sony Records release, which earned him a Grammy Award in 1984 for Best Children's Album. (*A Light in the Attic* got its own audio treatment in 1985.) Additional awards followed for several of his children's books, but his greatest prize that year was the birth of his son, Matthew.

By this time, Silverstein had become even more guarded about his personal life. He granted few, if any, invasions into his privacy, and almost nothing is known about Matthew's mother except that her name was Sarah Spencer and that she and Silverstein met in Key West sometime in the late 1970s. As with Susan Hastings, Silverstein did not enter into a long-term relationship with Spencer. They never married, nor did they live together for very long. Matthew's mother raised him primarily in Wisconsin.

THINGS CHANGE

Silverstein was almost 60 years old, but he still hid a few new tricks up his sleeve. Although he had written music for films, acted in them, and rubbed elbows with many of the best actors of his day, Silverstein had yet to write a screenplay until he and his friend David Mamet sat down to work on *Things Change*.

Mamet was coming in fresh from the successes of *The Untouchables*, which he had written for director Brian De Palma, and *House of Games*, which he had written and directed. Both films featured the hard-boiled dialogue and elaborate plot machinations that were quickly becoming trademarks of Mamet's work. The one thing the films lacked was a bit of texture in their characters—that intangible element of humanity that hooks an audience emotionally, grounds a plot in real life, and leaves a lasting impression.

Conversely, Silverstein did not have Mamet's technical expertise, but he did have a legendary sense of humor, plus an uncanny ability to distill an individual or situation to its essence. Together they came up with the character of Gino, an aging Chicago shoeshine man whose resemblance to a notorious Mafia boss gets him into a situation way over his head. Although it was not a blockbuster hit, *Things Change* was well received by critics and the public alike for its blend of comedy and drama, as well as the poignant portrayal of Gino by veteran actor Don Ameche.

Silverstein and Mamet teamed up again in 1989 to stage a pair of one-act plays in New York, first at the Mitzi E. Newhouse Theater on West 65th Street and later at Lincoln Center. The double bill, appearing under the umbrella title of *Oh, Hell*, was composed of one play by Mamet called *Billy Gould in Hell* and a second play by Silverstein called *The Devil and Billy Markham*. Silverstein drew inspiration for his play from a classic short story called "The Devil and Daniel Webster" by Stephen Vincent Benet. In the classic tradition of *Faust*, both plays concern deals with the devil gone wrong, as they always do.

The Devil and Billy Markham was originally published as a six-part epic poem in the January 1979 edition of *Playboy*.

It is essentially one long monologue in verse, in which a single narrator recounts the story of a cocky country singer who foolishly takes an impossible bet, and then compounds his error when he bets double-or-nothing. Silverstein tapped his old friend Dennis Locorriere, founding member of Dr. Hook and the Medicine Show, to perform the part; by most accounts, he was spellbinding. *Oh, Hell* played to a packed house for eight weeks running.

A critic at the time noted an inversion in the style of the plays delivered by Mamet and Silverstein.

> The most refreshing thing about *Oh, Hell* is the way each playwright seems to be working in the other's medium. After all, the world of pool halls and con games, where *Billy Markham* takes place, is Mamet's turf, just as obscenity has come to seem his special province. Nearly all the obscenity in *Oh, Hell* belongs to the Silverstein piece, all the whimsy to Mamet. It's as though the two men had agreed to swap souls for a term.[5]

Of all Silverstein's plays, *The Devil and Billy Markham* received the most critical attention. In 2006, it was revived for a successful run at the Algonquin Theater in New York.

Did you know...

David Mamet slipped a reference to his old friend Shel Silverstein into his 1997 film, *The Spanish Prisoner*. Toward the end, a little girl drops a book at the feet of Joe Ross, the protagonist played by Campbell Scott. It was a copy of *The Giving Tree*.

Silverstein poses with his guitar. Although he is perhaps best remembered as a children's book author, he also has numerous music credits to his name.

8

Falling Up and Checking Out

NOT CONTENT TO sit idle with a Grammy and a plethora of literary awards, Silverstein kicked off the 1990s with a Golden Globe Award and a "Best Song" nomination from the Academy of Motion Picture Arts and Sciences for "I'm Checking Out," a song he wrote for the 1990 film *Postcards From the Edge*. Meryl Streep actually sang the lyrics in the movie, and the exposure no doubt opened a lot of eyes and ears to the still-thriving talents of a tunesmith whose last hit song had been recorded nearly 15 years earlier.

Otherwise, Silverstein continued to focus primarily on playwriting. In June, the Ensemble Theater inaugurated its Marathon 1990 festival with his modern take on Shakespeare's *Hamlet*. The play, which set the action in urban America instead of feudal Denmark, featured Mario Van Peebles, who played all of the roles. It was later published in the January 1998 edition of *Playboy* as a long poem called "Hamlet as Told on the Street."

More plays followed from 1993 to 1994, and included *New Living Newspaper*, *The Lifeboat Is Sinking*, and a series of vignettes called *The Bed Plays* that premiered at a drama festival in Key West. The period was marred by sadness when, in May 1994, Silverstein's mother, Helen, died in Chicago at the age of 94.

THE GIVING TREE TURNS 30

In 1994, HarperCollins celebrated the thirtieth anniversary of the publication of *The Giving Tree* with a commemorative edition. The book proved as relevant and timely as ever, and it incited reactions from some surprising places. In early 1995, a periodical called *First Things* published by the Institute on Religion and Public Life organized and printed "The Giving Tree: A Symposium." Learned Harvard professors, rabbis, and the magazine's editor-in-chief all chimed in with different interpretations.

Although this was fascinating from a cultural standpoint, the various readings reveal more about the preconceptions and philosophies of the writers themselves than any inherent intent on Silverstein's part. Silverstein likely laughed at the idea that college professors would argue over his simple children's story, but the fact that it merited an argument at all probably pleased him. As he had said in an interview nearly 20 years earlier,

I would hope that people, no matter what age, would find something to identify with in my books, pick one up and experience a personal sense of discovery. That's great. But for them, not for me. I think if you're a creative person, you should just go about your business, do your work and not care about how it's received.[1]

THE AGING TECHNOPHOBE

After 15 years of pursuing other interests, Silverstein burst back onto the children's poetry scene in 1996 with the release of *Falling Up*, his third and final full-length collection. Just as many of the subjects explored in *A Light in the Attic* reflected Silverstein's transition from bawdy Uncle Shelby to a father figure more in tune with his adolescent readership, *Falling Up* reveals an author confronting middle age and the inexorable march of time.

A good number of poems are fixated on technology, and they express something akin to phobia with regard to its omnipresence in modern life. "Plugging In" points out what happens when you depend on electricity for everything, making it unforgettable to any contemporary kid who has had to suffer through a blackout. "Headphone Harold" not only hints at the social alienation that attends the use of such devices, but it also spins a tragic ending for its protagonist.

"Nope" warns about the frightening revelations that await anyone who uses science to look too closely at something as seemingly benign as a piece of cantaloupe. "My Robot" conveys, in terms a child can actually understand, the inevitable fallout from any advances in artificial intelligence. It also perfectly captures the frustration that anyone confounded by a technology they cannot control might feel. Conversely, "Remote-A-Dad" lampoons the manipulative

Above, Meryl Streep, who starred as Suzanne Vale, performs a song in the movie Postcards from Edge. *Silverstein wrote a song called "I'm Checking Out" for the movie, which won a Golden Globe award and a "Best Song" Oscar nomination.*

sense of entitlement and short attention span that is characteristic of nearly every American child born after the dawn
of MTV.

The poem that hits closest to home for Silverstein,
however, is "Writer Waiting." What good is all this new-
fangled gadgetry, the poem asks, if it does not make us
more creative? A computer may be able to make us better
spellers, help us tidy up our type, or streamline the work
process, but it cannot write anything for us. That part is
still up to the human. This idea is linked directly to the
main themes of *Where the Sidewalks Ends* and *A Light in
the Attic*. In Silverstein's worldview, the imagination is
still the most important tool at any child's disposal. Without it, both the machines and the humans are useless.

Elsewhere in *Falling Up*, Silverstein betrays growing
concerns about aging and death, first hinted at with "The
Little Boy and the Old Man" from *A Light in the Attic*.
"Scale" tackles the common worry of weight gain; "The
Folks Inside" cautions children to make the most of their
youth, because old age comes for everybody; and the
promise of reincarnation in "Stork Story" seems to be
made as much for the poet's benefit as any of his much
younger readers.

Falling Up does not exclusively concern itself with the
fears of an aging technophobe, though. There are plenty
of poems sympathetic to the various plights of children
("Unfair," "No Grownups"), gruesome fantasies ("Head-
less Town," "Foot Repair"), and the requisite tall tales
about colorful characters ("Allison Beals and Her 25 Eels,"
"Reachin' Richard," and "Screamin' Millie," among others).
Yet another "Diving Board" poem proves that Silverstein
finds that motif endlessly fascinating. Even old Uncle

Shelby still has his fun, with poems like "Dancin' in the Rain," "Tell Me," and "Tattooin' Ruth," accompanied by drawings of naked characters, not to mention the trademark flasher in the index whose beard is now long enough to cover nearly four pages. American society had become quite a bit more permissive since *A Light in the Attic* was published, and these minor transgressions came off as more funny than shocking, which is probably how Silverstein wanted it, anyway.

There are more illustrations overall in *Falling Up* than in *Attic* or *Sidewalk,* as well as less blank space. Almost every poem has an illustration, and the drawings themselves tend to be a bit more detailed. Perhaps Silverstein sensed that the children of 1996 needed more visual stimuli than their predecessors, or he may have decided that *Falling Up* would be his last collection and wanted to fit as much of his artwork in there as possible. We will never know for sure, but on the final page, just inside the back cover, there is a curious hand-printed message from Silverstein to his readers: "The end of the book— / No use to look / For any more, my dear, / 'Cause if you try finding / some more in the binding, / You may just . . . disappear. Bye-bye, S.S." All in all, *Falling Up* represents neither a departure nor a retread of Silverstein's previous collections, but rather a natural progression and satisfying conclusion to his career as America's best-loved children's poet.

MURDER, HE WROTE

Shel Silverstein had set out to be a professional cartoonist. He achieved that goal before his twenty-fifth year. An old friend (Tomi Ungerer) suggested he write children's books, and the rest is history. Another friend (Bob Gibson) said he should try to write songs, and so, over the next 40 years, he wrote nearly 800 of them. One earned its performer (Johnny Cash) a Grammy. Another earned Silverstein an Oscar nomination. A dozen more were chart-topping hits. When he was not writing poems, stories, or songs, he wrote critically acclaimed plays. If any modern American can justly be labeled a Renaissance man, then surely that man is Shel Silverstein.

It should therefore come as no surprise that, when another close friend named Otto Penzler asked him to try his hand at crime fiction, Silverstein simply sat down and delivered. Penzler was a mystery-bookstore owner and a well-known figure in the genre. In 1996, he published a collection of short stories called *Murder for Love* that featured contributions by the best-known writers in the field. It also included a devastating little piece entitled "For What She Had Done" by Silverstein. Written in a kind of free verse, it tells a morbid fable of murder that purports, with Silverstein's trademark black humor, to explain how the tradition of giving flower bouquets originated. Penzler introduced the piece with yet another testament to Silverstein's endless creativity:

> For anyone who ever dreamed of creating stories, or poems, of drawing, or writing songs and plays, but couldn't quite find the originality of expression that set them apart from the pedestrian, Shel Silverstein is their worst nightmare.
>
> When he is asked to write the lyrics of a song, he needs no more than 15 minutes. A play might need an entire weekend. When I asked him to write a story for this book, he said, "Well, I've never written a crime story in my life. Wait, I have an idea." He never paused for breath between those two sentences.[2]

Penzler went on to publish two more anthologies: *Murder for Revenge* (1998) and *Murder for Obsession* (1999), both with contributions from Silverstein.

OLD DOGS

Death must have preoccupied Silverstein during this period, particularly after he buried his good friend Bob Gibson. Gibson was suffering from progressive supranuclear palsy (PSP), an affliction of the brain and nervous system akin to Alzheimer's or Parkinson's disease. Doctors could do nothing for him, so friends and family decided to celebrate his life and work while he was still around to enjoy it. The resulting event, including a concert and a party, was held in Chicago in September 1996. Many of Gibson's contemporaries were on hand to pay tribute, along with a few Chicago celebrities, including Roger McGuinn (of the Byrds), Peter Yarrow (of Peter, Paul, and Mary), Studs Terkel, Roger Ebert, and of course, Shel Silverstein. Gibson died a week later at his home in Portland.

Although Gibson never achieved the kind of stardom and household name recognition shared by many of his friends, the words to a song Silverstein wrote for him called "The Living Legend" remain a poignant reminder of a man who faced a hard life with courage and dignity: "So I take the love of them who still remember / Take the help of them who care to give / Swap my songs for sandwiches and shelter / Even living legends got to live. . . ."

As Bob Gibson's case proved, Silverstein and his contemporaries were not getting any younger, but they still had plenty of fire in them. It was in that spirit that four aging country and western legends—Bobby Bare, Waylon Jennings, Mel Tillis, and Jerry Reed—decided to call themselves the Old Dogs and record an album's worth of songs by Silverstein in 1998. The record, also called *Old Dogs*, is a hilarious rumination on heading over the hill, set to the old-school twang of steel guitars and bar-room harmonies. Songs like "I Never Expected" and "Still Gonna Die" proved that Silverstein may have been worried about his own mortality, as well as everyone else's, but he still planned to go out with a grin on his face. As he himself put it in the liner notes, "I've never had more fun in my life."

CHECKING OUT

Shel Silverstein died without warning. Two cleaning women found his body on Monday, May 10, 1999, in the bedroom of his Key West home. It was later determined that he had suffered a massive heart attack on the Saturday or Sunday before he was found. It is possible that he died while he was writing. He was 68 years old.

Everyone who knew him was blindsided by his death. Bobby Bare, who had spoken with Silverstein on the phone the night before he died, would later say that the words "dead" and "Shel Silverstein" were simply incompatible. Over the following days and weeks, many friends and acquaintances wrote obituaries for him; they all emphasized what a pleasure it was to know him, what a creative genius he was, and what a tremendous void his death had left. Several of his closest friends privately published a book of remembrance in his honor.

Silverstein was survived by his sister Peggy, who became the manager of his literary affairs, and his son Matthew, who inherited an estate worth somewhere between $15 and $20 million.

POST HUMOROUS

Silverstein's passing did not mean that his fans had seen the last of him or his work. Several projects were already in the works at the time of his death. In late 1999, an album full of songs about truckers and trucking called *Kickin' Asphalt* was released. Silverstein had penned 8 of the 21 tracks, which were performed by veteran country singers. In 2000, his friend Fred Koller entered the studio and recorded an album of songs the pair had written together over the years, entitled *No Song Left to Sell*. Released by Gadfly Records in mid 2001, it featured quite a few songs that might otherwise have been lost to history.

In fall 2001, David Mamet culled 10 of his friend's best one-act plays and staged them at the Atlantic Theater Company (a New York playhouse he cofounded in 1985), calling it *An Adult Evening of Shel Silverstein*. One-act plays are often staged only once as part of a themed production or festival. By assembling this body of work into a more unified whole, Mamet single-handedly preserved Silverstein's playwriting legacy, gave it

Did you know...

Shel Silverstein was inducted into the Nashville Songwriters Hall of Fame on November 4, 2002, the same night as Bob Dylan. Bobby Bare sang a few of Silverstein's songs and gave the induction speech, concluding with the lines: "We've got to ask ourselves. Did [Silverstein] leave too early or have we stayed too late?"

greater substance, and made it more attractive for other drama troupes to perform. As a result, in the years since its debut, *An Adult Evening of Shel Silverstein* has been staged many times, in theaters all over the country.

Shel Silverstein may have moved on from this world, but he did not abandon his young fans. In fact, the last project he signed off on before his death was a CD and illustrated booklet entitled *Underwaterland*, which appeared in October 2002. Seventeen silly songs introduce children to a whole host of memorable sea creatures, from "Bubble Barracuda" to "Captain Octopus." Pat Dailey, a musician Silverstein met and befriended in Key West in the early 1980s when Dailey was performing at Sloppy Joe's Bar, performed the songs. A troupe of Nashville musicians accompanied Dailey, and Silverstein himself sings along on several tracks, as well as providing a 32-page booklet full of lyrics and illustrations. *Underwaterland* earned its creators a Parent's Choice Gold Award and the Parent's Guide to Children's Media Award.

In 2004, a thirtieth-anniversary edition of *Where the Sidewalk Ends* was published, which includes 12 new poems. In the same year, a limited fortieth-anniversary edition of *The Giving Tree* appeared, with a CD containing a recording of Silverstein reading the book.

The most recent entirely new work by Silverstein is *Runny Babbit*, a small collection of poems published in 2005 in which the first letter or syllable of many word pairs are switched. These are generally known as spoonerisms, after a nineteenth-century English reverend named William Archibald Spooner, who was prone to such slips of the tongue. Technically speaking, spoonerisms involve real words (for example, "wave the sails" instead of "save the whales"), but Silverstein did not constrain himself that way. The result is a tongue-twisting laugh fest that tickles the brain while it challenges our fixed notions of language.

According to his nephew Mitch Myers, who had a major hand in seeing the project through to publication in 2005, Silverstein had worked on *Runny Babbit* on and off for more than 25 years; shortly before his death, Silverstein created a dedication page to his friend "Marry Loyer" (Larry Moyer), which indicated that the book was completed. The time period between the author's death and the eventual release of *Runny Babbit* is a testament to the family's respect for Silverstein's legacy, as well as the care with which they handle his affairs. Given Silverstein's notorious habit of writing and doodling on every scrap of paper he could find, one can only hope that other works of this caliber lie hidden among his effects, awaiting their time in the sun.

One thing is certain: No further publications are necessary to secure Silverstein's place in the pantheon of America's most creative minds. It might come as a surprise to his fans to learn that, despite Silverstein's penchant for informal attire, his alternative lifestyle and, most of all, his tireless rebellion against all forms of authority, he was a perfectionist. Silverstein knew what every great artist knows: that ultimately what survives is the work you leave behind. This careful attention to detail shines through mostly clearly in his books for children. All of his books share a common, hallmark look, and none (save *Uncle Shelby's ABZ Book*) has ever appeared in any format other than hardback. In an age of throwaway culture, when 15 minutes of fame is more than most people can hope for, Shel Silverstein left a body of work that will entertain children—and adults—for generations to come.

CHRONOLOGY

1930 Sheldon Allan Silverstein is born in Chicago, Illinois, to Nathan and Helen Silverstein.

1948 Silverstein graduates from Roosevelt High School.

1949 Silverstein is dismissed after one year of study at University of Illinois at Navy Pier.

1950 Silverstein studies for one year at Chicago Academy of Fine Arts.

1950–1953 Silverstein completes three years of coursework at Roosevelt University, in Chicago.

1953 Silverstein is drafted into U.S. Army in September; he serves in Japan and Korea; he begins to publish daily cartoons for Pacific edition of *Stars and Stripes*.

1956 Silverstein begins to draw cartoons for *Playboy*.

1959 First music album, *Hairy Jazz*, is released.

1962 *Inside Folk Songs* is released.

1965 *I'm So Good That I Don't Have to Brag* is released.

1967 *Drain My Brain* is released.

1968 *Dirty Feet* (book collection of music and lyrics) is released.

1969 Record LP, *A Boy Named Sue and His Other Country Songs* is released; Johnny Cash performs "A Boy Named Sue" at San Quentin prison.

1970 Daughter Shoshanna is born to Silverstein and Susan Hastings; Silverstein writes original motion picture score for *Ned Kelly*.

1971 Silverstein writes score for *Who Is Harry Kellerman and Why Is He Saying Those Terrible Things About Me?*; Silverstein begins collaboration with Dr. Hook and the Medicine Show.

1972 *Freakin' at the Freakers Ball* album is released.

1975 Girlfriend Susan Hastings, Shoshanna's mother, dies in Baltimore, Maryland.

1977 Silverstein writes film score for *Thieves*.

1978 *Songs & Stories* album is released.

1979 *Different Dances* is published.

1980 *The Great Conch Train Robbery* is released.

1981 *A Light in the Attic* is published; and wins the *School Library Journal* Best Books for Children Award; first play, *The Lady or the Tiger Show*, is performed.

1982 Daughter Shoshanna dies of a brain aneurysm in Baltimore, Maryland.

1983 *Gorilla* and *Wild Life* are performed.

1984 *Remember Crazy Zelda?* is performed; Silverstein wins Grammy for his recording of *Where The Sidewalk Ends*; son Matthew is born.

1985 *The Happy Hour*; *The Crate*; *One Tennis Shoe*; *Wash and Dry*; and *Very Very Serious Plays* are performed.

1986 *Happy Endings*; *Little Feet*; and *The Empty Room* are performed.

1988 Collaborates with David Mamet on screenplay for film *Things Change*.

1996 *Falling Up* is published; Silverstein nominated for Academy Award for his song "I'm Checking Out" from film *Postcards from the Edge*; Silverstein writes "murder poem" for Otto Penzler's *Murder for Love*.

1998 *The Trio* is performed; Silverstein writes words and music for *Old Dogs* album; Silverstein contributes two more pieces to Penzler's follow-up collections *Murder for Revenge* and *Murder for Obsession*.

1999 Silverstein dies of heart failure in Key West, Florida, on May 10; *Kickin' Asphalt* album is released, with eight songs by Silverstein.

2001 David Mamet produces "An Adult Evening of Shel Silverstein" featuring 10 of Silverstein's one-act plays.

2002 *Underwaterland* CD is released; Silverstein inducted into Country Music Songwriter's Hall of Fame.

2005 Last new book, *Runny Babbit,* is published.

NOTES

Chapter 1

1 Jean Mercier, "Shel Silverstein," *Publishers Weekly*. (February 24, 1975): pp. 50–52.

2 Shel Silverstein, "Introduction," in *Grab Your Socks! New Army Cartoons*. New York: Ballantine, 1956.

3 Hal Drake, "Cartoonist Silverstein Called Stripes His Catapult to Success," *Stars and Stripes*. (October 1, 1995).

4 Jeff Begun, ed., "Interview With Shel Silverstein," *Aardvark*. (Fall, 1963).

5 Robert D. Sweeney, "Introduction," in Shel Silverstein, *Take Ten*. Tokyo: Powell, 1955.

6 Shel Silverstein, "Introduction."

7 Jean Shepard, in *Hairy Jazz* (album liner notes). New York: Elektra Records, 1959.

8 Ruth MacDonald, *Shel Silverstein*. New York: Twayne, 1997, pp. 2–3.

9 Jean Shepard, "Introduction," in Shel Silverstein, *Now Here's My Plan: A Book of Futilities*. New York: Simon and Schuster, 1960.

10 Ibid.

Chapter 2

1 Mercier, "Shel Silverstein," pp. 50–52.

2 Leonard S. Marcus, ed., *Dear Genius: The Letters of Ursula Nordstrom*. New York: HarperCollins, 1998, p. xix.

3 Ibid., p. xvii.

4 Ibid., p. 27.

Chapter 3

1 Mary Ann Glendon, "*The Giving Tree*: A Symposium," *First Things*. (January 1995).

2 Rik Elswit, "A Boy Named Shel." May 27, 1999. http://www.salon.com.

3 Richard R. Lingeman, "The Third Mr. Silverstein," *New York Times Book Review*. (April 30, 1978): p. 57.

4 Ibid.

5 William Cole, "About Alice, a Rabbit, a Tree," *New York Times Book Review*. (September 9, 1973).

6 Leonard S. Marcus, ed, *Dear Genius: The Letters of Ursula Nordstrom*. New York: HarperCollins, 1998, p. 372.

7 William Cole, "About Alice, a Rabbit, a Tree," *New York Times Book Review*. (September 9, 1973).

Chapter 4

1 Al Rickets, *Tokyo Weekender*. (May 21, 1999).

2 Lynn Van Matre, "Breaking Open Silverstein's Shell," *Chicago Tribune.* (March 4, 1973).

3 Paul Zollo, "In the Shade of the Giving Tree," *Performing Songwriter.* July–August, 1999.

4 Ibid.

5 William Cole, in *Inside Folk Songs* (album liner notes). New York: Atlantic Records, 1962.

6 Shel Silverstein, *I'm So Good That I Don't Have to Brag* (album liner notes). Chicago: Cadet Records, 1965.

7 Herb Gardner, in *Drain My Brain* (album liner notes). Chicago: Cadet Records, 1966.

8 Van Matre, "Breaking Open Silverstein's Shell."

9 Lingeman, "The Third Mr. Silverstein," p. 57.

10 Elswit, "A Boy Named Shel."

11 Tim Cahill, "Dr. Hook's VD and Medicine Shows," *Rolling Stone.* (November 9, 1972).

12 Ibid.

13 "Fred Koller & Shel Silverstein." http://www.fredkoller.com.

14 Shel Silverstein, "Introduction," *Uncle Shelby's ABZ Book.* New York: Simon & Schuster, 1961.

Chapter 5

1 Rickets, *Tokyo Weekender.*

2 Marcus, *Dear Genius*, p. 255.

3 Elswit, "A Boy Named Shel."

4 Marcus, *Dear Genius,* p. 255.

5 Ibid., p. 367.

6 MacDonald, pp. 42–43.

Chapter 6

1 Lingeman, "The Third Mr. Silverstein," p. 57.

2 MacDonald, *Shel Silverstein,* p. 77.

3 Ibid., pp. 77–78.

4 Ibid., p. 80.

Chapter 7

1 "The Magical World of Shel Silverstein," *Playboy.* (January 2006): pp. 74–78, 151–153.

2 David Mamet, "Shel Silverstein: A Friend Who Lived Life the Chicago Way." *New York Times.* (October 14, 2001): p. 27.

3 Ibid.

4 Ibid.

5 Mimi Kruger, "Double or Nothing," *New Yorker.* (December 25, 1989).

Chapter 8

1 Mercier, "Shel Silverstein," p. 52.

2 Otto Penzler, "Introduction," *Murder for Love.* New York: Bantam Dell, 1996.

WORKS BY
SHEL SILVERSTEIN

1955 *Take Ten* (collection of army cartoons)

1960 *Now Here's My Plan: A Book of Futilities*

1961 *Uncle Shelby's ABZ Book: A Primer for Tender Young Minds*

1963 *A Playboy's Teevee Jeebies*; *Lafcadio, the Lion Who Shot Back*

1964 *The Giving Tree*; *A Giraffe and a Half*; *Uncle Shelby's Zoo: Don't Bump the Glump!*; *Who Wants a Cheap Rhinoceros?*

1965 *More Playboy's Teevee Jeebies: Do-It-Yourself Dialogue for the Late Late Show*

1974 *Where the Sidewalk Ends*

1976 *The Missing Piece*

1981 *The Missing Piece Meets the Big O*; *A Light in the Attic*

1996 *Falling Up*

2002 *Underwaterland* (book and CD)

2005 *Runny Babbit* (published posthumously)

POPULAR BOOKS

THE GIVING TREE
> A young boy develops a friendship with a tree. As the boy grows older, he takes more and more from the tree, and gives less of himself, but the tree is happy to give what she can.

WHERE THE SIDEWALK ENDS
> This is a collection of mostly humorous short poems that are illustrated by Silverstein with black-and-white line drawings.

THE MISSING PIECE
> A circular-shaped character named It sets out to look for its missing piece, and discovers that it is more interesting to search for the piece than to actually find it.

A LIGHT IN THE ATTIC
> The follow-up to *Where the Sidewalk Ends* is a similar volume of poetry for children.

POPULAR CHARACTERS

LAFCADIO

In Silverstein's first children's book, *Lafcadio, the Lion Who Shot Back*, Lafcadio the lion leaves the jungle and lives like a man for a while.

THE GIVING TREE & THE BOY

In *The Giving Tree*, one of Silverstein's signature books, these two characters are portrayed as opposites. One gives; the other takes.

JIMMY JET

The title character of the poem "Jimmy Jet and His TV Set" (from *Where the Sidewalk Ends*) watches TV all night and day until he turns into a TV himself.

SARAH CYNTHIA SYLVIA STOUT

The young girl described in the poem "Sarah Cynthia Sylvia Stout Would Not Take the Garbage Out" (*Where the Sidewalk Ends*) is punished for her refusal to do her chores by an enormous, stinking pile of garbage.

PAMELA PURSE

The girl in the poem "Ladies First" (from *A Light in the Attic*) proclaims that girls should go first to the consternation of everyone around her, until it gets her into trouble with a very hungry lion.

MAJOR AWARDS

1974 *Where the Sidewalk Ends* is selected for a *New York Times* Notable Book Award.

1981 *Where the Sidewalk Ends* is selected for a Michigan Young Readers Award. *A Light in the Attic* is selected as one of *School Library Journal's* Best Books.

1982 *The Missing Piece Meets the Big O* receives an International Reading Association's Children's Choice Award.

1983 *A Light in the Attic* receives a Buckeye Children's Book Award, in which children in the state of Ohio nominate and then vote on their favorite books each year.

1984 *Where the Sidewalk Ends* and *A Light in the Attic* are selected for a George G. Stone Award. *A Light in the Attic* receives a William Allen White Award.

1985 *A Light in the Attic* receives a second Buckeye Award.

BIBLIOGRAPHY

Cahill, Tim. "Dr. Hook's VD and Medicine Shows." *Rolling Stone* (November 9, 1972).

Cole, William. "About Alice, a Rabbit, a Tree." *New York Times Book Review* (September 9, 1973).

Drake, Hal. "Cartoonist Silverstein called Stripes His Catapult to Success." *Stars and Stripes* (October 1, 1995).

Elswit, Rik. "A Boy Named Shel." Available online. URL: http://www.salon.com/people/feature/1999/05/27/shel/index.html. May 27, 1999.

Freedman, Samuel J. "Two Authors Venture Into Alien Land of Theater." *New York Times* (February 8, 1985): p. C4.

Glendon, Mary Ann. "*The Giving Tree*: A Symposium." *First Things* (January 1995): pp. 22–45.

Kennedy, X.J. "A Rhyme Is a Chime." *New York Times Book Review* (November 15, 1981): p. 51.

Kruger, Mimi. "Double or Nothing." *New Yorker* (December 25, 1989).

Lingeman, Richard R. "The Third Mr. Silverstein." *New York Times Book Review* (April 30, 1978): p. 57.

Livingston, Myra Cohn. "The Light in His Attic." *New York Times Book Review* (March 9, 1986): pp. 36–37.

Mamet, David. "Shel Silverstein: A Friend Who Lived Life the Chicago Way." *New York Times* (October 14, 2001).

Mercier, Jean. "Shel Silverstein." *Publishers Weekly* (February 24, 1975): pp. 50–52.

Myers, Mitch. "Shel Silverstein: 1930–1999." *Rolling Stone* (June 24, 1999): p. 26.

Rickets, Al. *Tokyo Weekender* (May 21, 1999).

Rogak, Lisa. "Shel Games." Available online. URL: http://www.salon.com. April 20, 2005.

Sarah Weinman's Shel Silverstein Archive. Available online. URL: http://members.tripod.com/~ShelSilverstein/.

"Shel Silverstein: The Aardvark Interview." *Aardvark* (Autumn, 1963).

Silverstein, Shel. Interview by Studs Terkel. WFMT, December 6, 1961 and December 12, 1963.

Van Matre, Lynn. "Breaking Open Silverstein's Shell." *Chicago Tribune* (March 4, 1973).

Zollo, Paul. "In the Shade of the Giving Tree." *Performing Songwriter* (July–August, 1999).

FURTHER READING

MacDonald, Ruth. *Shel Silverstein*. New York: Twayne, 1997.

Marcus, Leonard S., ed. *Dear Genius: The Letters of Ursula Nordstrom*. New York: HarperCollins, 1998.

Rogak, Lisa. *A Boy Named Shel: The Life and Times of Shel Silverstein*. New York: Thomas Dunne Books, 2007.

Web Sites

Shel Silverstein
www.shelsilverstein.com

Sarah Weinman's Shel Silverstein Archive
http://shelsilverstein.tripod.com

Shel Silverstein: Collected Information by Sely Friday
http://www.nassio.com/silverstein/

Shel Silverstein Bibliography of Children's Books.
http://falcon.jmu.edu/~ramseyil/silversteinbib.htm

All Music Guide Entry on Shel Silverstein.
http://www.allmusic.com/cg/amg.dll

PICTURE CREDITS

INDEX

ABOUT THE CONTRIBUTOR

MICHAEL GRAY BAUGHAN is a freelance author and researcher. When he is not glued to his computer, he can usually be found running around after his rambunctious twin daughters, Callie and Ella. In addition to the present volume, he has written a biography of Charles Bukowski, as well as study guides to the work of e.e. cummings, Rudyard Kipling, and John Ashbery.

Need to Renew?
Call the Library at
985-2173.

DATE DUE

	2009		
MAR 1 7 2009			
May 10			
MAY 2009			

DEMCO 38-296